Praise for Become a Business Money Magnet™

'A book that makes business finance accessible and empowering! Transformative advice that offers invaluable insights and actionable strategies.'

Lisa Messenger
Founder & CEO of Collective Hub. Best Selling Author of over 2 million copies of her products.

'Finally, an honest and practical guide to overcoming money fears and creating a high profit business.'

Kate Toon
Founder – Stay Tooned
Author | Six Figures in School Hours | Six Figures While You Sleep

'Justine explains the fundamentals of business finance in a simple and easy to follow way; a must-read for anyone in business.'

Molly Benjamin
Founder – Ladies Finance Club

'If numbers are not your thing – or even if they are – this is THE business bible you need to transform your financial position.'

Sarah Megginson
Personal Finance Expert – Writer – Head of Editorial Finder.com.au

'A must-read for any one in business wanting to make more money. Justine makes business money accessible, understandable and most of all achievable.'

Rebecca Saunders
Serial Entrepreneur & Global Speaker
Founder of The Champagne Lounge

'Become a Business Money Magnet^{TM}' is the book I wish I had when starting my business. Even now, 10 years into my entrepreneurship journey, I found it to be so full of valuable insights, practical tips and transformative lessons. Justine is like your own personal money mentor who is here to help you succeed.'

Maha Corbett
Co-Founder, SWIISH

'Become a Business Money Magnet^{TM}' is the perfect guide to take you from money novice to money master – and a worthwhile investment for your business.'

Colleen Callander
Founder of Mentor Me
Author – Speaker – Business & Leadership Coach

'Even if you think you just don't have a head for the numbers, Justine's book shows you why every business owner can and should get to grips with the basics. You may even start to enjoy it!'

Jen Bishop
Founder & Publisher
The Interiors Addict

'Simple, practical, brilliant! A must read!'

Shannah Kennedy
Life Strategist, Wellbeing Specialist, 8 x Best-selling author

Justine's book is like having a financial mentor by your side. Insightful, relatable, and packed with wisdom, it's a game-changer for business owners who want to be financially fit and have longevity in their business.'

Laura Robinson
Compass Copywriting – SEO Copywriter

'Justine McLean's 'Become A Business Money Magnet^{TM}' should be mandatory reading for all business owners. Her approachable attitude towards business finances helps anyone who's had their head in the sand too long about the financial health of their business and is ready to take action.'

Emma Blomfield
Director & Principal Stylist – Emma Blomfield Studio

'Justine has a powerful message to share about money and the power of taking control of your business finances. Hearing Justine's story and how she used a very stressful financial circumstance to catalyse such a transformation in her approach to money is inspiring. The good news is that we don't need to become a certified BAS Agent ourselves to gain this level of control – Justine has done the hard work to translate what business owners need to know into an easy-to-digest read that we can use to take action on our own finances.'

Kerry Rowett
Reiki Master

'"Become a Business Money Magnet^{TM}" is the book I wish I had when I was starting out in business 14 years ago. Justine's sage advice, practical guidance and business savvy are a must for any entrepreneur to set up a sound money foundation. This book will help you go from surviving to thriving.'

Emma Lovell
Business Travel Life Coach

'Reading "Become A Business Money Magnet^{TM}" felt like having a conversation with a trusted friend. Justine brings a wealth of knowledge and makes financial concepts easy to comprehend. This is a must-read for anyone serious about their finances and business success.'

Sheree Rubinstein
Founder of One Roof

'This book would have helped me improve my financial literacy, build confidence in my own abilities to run a profitable business, understand the money stuff that matters (and the stuff that's just a distraction) and get out of my own way to become a total money boss.

I had to learn the hard way, but thanks to Justine, you don't have to. This is the ultimate cheat-sheet to becoming a profitable business bod.'

Erin Huckle
Chuckle Communications

Become a Business Money Magnet™

Simple habits to manage your money and supercharge your profits

Justine McLean

The Rural Publishing Company

First published by The Rural Publishing Company 2024.

Copyright © 2024 Justine McLean

Print (Paperback): 978-1-923008-24-3
eBook: 978-1-923008-25-0

Cover Design: The Rural Publishing Company
Typesetting & Design: The Rural Publishing Company

The Rural
Publishing Company

The Rural Publishing Company
Website: https://theruralpublishingcompany.com.au
Email: hello@theruralpublishingcompany.com.au

Dedication

For David, Love of my life.
Thank you for believing in me even when I didn't.

To my boys Benjamin, Lachlan, Ryan and Jackson
I love you! You complete me!

To Buddy, Lute, Milo and Lily who keep me smiling!

Disclaimer

The information provided in this book is general in nature.

While we have made every effort to include current and accurate information in this publication and associated materials, Flossi Creative Pty Ltd and its employees, and The Rural Publishing Company accepts no responsibility for the accuracy or completeness of any information included or any loss or damage that occurs by using this information. We recommend that users exercise care with respect to its use.

In addition, as we are not aware of your personal circumstances, financial position, objectives or the specifics of your business, please consider the information carefully and decide if it is appropriate to your business and personal circumstances before proceeding.

We encourage you to seek further, professional advice if necessary and before making any business or personal decisions.

*All names of clients and their businesses featured in the case studies in this book have been changed to protect privacy.

Contents

Foreword

By Kate Toon

Money. It's a funny old thing.

We want more of it, but we don't want to be slaves to it.

Some of us love talking about it and others feel awkward or embarrassed when anything financial comes up. That's because money represents different things for each of us: freedom, security, choice, abundance ... it's scary, wonderful, depressing, and glorious all at the same time.

My relationship with money has changed a lot over the years. From a working/middle class background with a 'save' mentality – money has always been a dull throb in the back of my mind. A lack of it meant eating beans on toast for most of my college years, and not pursuing my dream career. Mismanagement of it led to massive angst-ridden debt in my 20s. And as a small business owner, I've white knuckled the rollercoaster of feast and famine with the best of them.

Then all of a sudden, I got some money but I still didn't feel well off.

It wasn't until I took the time to educate myself that things changed – I could have done with this book back then. If I had I think I would have been able to:

1. Grasp my finances faster and just understand all the weird terms and reports much sooner.

2. Be more confident about making big financial decisions – I was so nervous to spend money and that held me back.

3. Work harder at profitability – because for me that's the real key to being a money magnet.

Sure, I had an accountant who I trusted to do the right thing (spoiler – they didn't). And yes, I had financial software that spat out glorious reports (that I couldn't understand).

But even after several years in business I was still stumbling around blindly in the financial dark. And like Justine, I racked up a fat debt with the tax man. Over the last several years I've dragged myself from the financially incompetent pit using many of the tactics Justine covers in the book, including:

1. Being aware of my self-limiting beliefs around money.

2. Creating financial plans.

3. Creating a Profit First style envelope system with different bank accounts.

4. Surrounding myself with smart money people.

5. Asking daft questions.

6. Considering cash flow.

7. Focusing on profitability rather than revenue.

8. Upping my prices and valuing myself.

I used to tell myself the story that I was a words person and therefore not good with figures. Now, I'm good with both. In fact, I like to think

I'm a bit of a money magnet. As Justine explains so well in the following pages, it's not just about setting up a 'Money Monday' or 'Finance Friday', it's about shifting your whole attitude to money. Embracing it, loving it, removing emotion and taking practical action. Getting your finances in order and creating balance is, as Justine explains, a lot of work initially. But it doesn't take long for the habits to stick and new positive financial neural pathways to form. By following the strategies in this book, you'll set up solid foundations, improve your confidence and be able to turn that money frown upside down.

'Become a Business Money Magnet™' is an honest and practical guide to overcoming money fears and creating a high profit business and is a great investment for your business.

Enjoy.

Kate Toon
Founder – Stay Tooned
Author | Six Figures in School Hours | Six Figures While You Sleep

Chapter 1

How a 5-Figure Tax Debt Changed My Life

'Do the best you can until you know better. Then when you know better, do better'.

Maya Angelou – Poet, Author, Activist

What comes to mind when I say forty-two thousand dollars?

For most of us, it's a significant, life-changing number, especially if the money lands in your bank account. But what if that forty-two thousand dollars was a debt, rather than a windfall?

That number, $42,000, took me to the edge. It made me question my competence, my ability and my choices. It filled me with doubt, made me feel powerless and stupid, and forced me to question every single decision I'd made in my business.

But it wasn't all negative. It also helped me shine a spotlight on myself, my business and how I dealt with money. That number could have ruined me, my relationship, my family and my business, but instead, it changed my life forever – and probably not in the way you'd expect.

The $42,000 in question was a tax debt, rather than a windfall. After only our second year in business, we were in hock to the Australian Tax Office (ATO) for $42k and at the time, we didn't have a single cent set aside to pay the debt off.

But before I tell you how our $42,000 debt changed our lives, I need to go back a few years and set the scene. The year was 1994, and I'd just given birth to my first son, Ben. After a few months at home, I realised I didn't want to return to work full-time in the publishing industry. I wanted to stay home and raise my baby.

Financially, however, I needed to work. We had a mortgage with a 7.5 percent interest rate, and we'd just come out of 'the recession we had to have', so relying on one income was a luxury we couldn't afford. At the time, the freelance economy wasn't what it is today and there was absolutely no working from home.

Undeterred, I approached the 'men in suits' at the publishing firm where I worked and suggested a bit of a hybrid arrangement: I'd work as a freelancer, a few days in the office and a few days working from home. To say they were horrified is an understatement. Fortunately, I had a secret weapon up my sleeve: six fabulous authors who refused to work without my help, so my employer had to agree to my 'strange' working hybrid. I became one of the first freelancers employed at the publishing company and created my first business.

I knew very little about running my own business, as I'd always been an employee up to that point. But my first foray into the business world was simple, really; essentially, I was trading time for money, so I decided to jump in feet first and wing it. I did the work and billed my hours. And that worked well for me.

Roll forward a few years and four children later, and I had the business bug. My freelance business had expanded and was doing well. I was still trading time for money, but now I had more expenses, more clients, and way less time. I mean four children! The juggle was relentless, and I was exhausted.

So, over the Christmas holidays in 2001, I suggested to my husband that we think about starting a business together – a brick-and-mortar retail toy store and e-commerce site.

I wanted our shop to be a destination store. One inspired by the store in the *Shop Around The Corner*, where the neighbourhood kids could come and hear stories, celebrate birthdays, be entertained and their parents could buy the best quality toys on the market. I must've made a good case because David, a risk-averse kind of guy and General Manager of a major airline's Sydney base, loved the idea.

So, we bought a book on how to start a business and began researching locations. We talked about the sort of business we wanted to put together, what products we wanted to stock, who our ideal client was, and how much money we could make; we even put together a business budget. We had the money to fund the store, so we took a leap of faith and, in early 2002, we opened our doors in a leafy suburb on the northern beaches in Sydney.

Now, as you do when you go into business with your partner, you divide up all of the jobs, and that's what we did. My husband decided that he wanted to work in the store in a customer-facing role. I wanted to do the buying and merchandising, make everything look pretty, and also put together the arts and crafts classes and all the creative elements of the business.

Of course, there were many other 'little' things to do, like the marketing and finances, but we didn't make any big decisions about who would do those upfront. However, somewhere along the line, I got stuck with the numbers; I'm not even sure when it happened. And that's saying something because, honestly, I didn't do numbers. I wasn't great at maths at school, and it wasn't my sweet spot.

Experts to the rescue …

Because I knew very little about business finance, I thought the best thing to do was consult an expert. So, I asked around and hired an accountant. The accountant suggested we get an Australian Business Number, told me about the relevant taxes and how to register and said they would see us at tax time, and that was the end of that.

After a conversation with a bookkeeper friend, I realised I needed to do more regarding business finances than get an ABN, register for taxes and wait for tax time. So, I took her advice, bought some cloud accounting software called MYOB, and decided I could do the rest myself.

It very quickly became apparent I needed help. I was an *awful* bookkeeper!

As a new business, we'd decided to bootstrap rather than borrow, so hiring outside help was a big decision. On the one hand, it was an investment we couldn't really afford as such a new business. On the other hand, a good bookkeeper would make all the difference and get our finances on track …

We decided to hire someone. And now, with a bookkeeper and accountant on board, I felt like I could check finances off my list. Which is exactly what I did – I completely abdicated my financial responsibility to the business. 'They could handle it', I thought. 'I'll see them at tax time'.

It was one of the best business decisions I'd made in my short business career, right?

Wrong. It turned out to be one of the worst and costliest mistakes I would make, and things went pear-shaped quickly.

Turns out, the bookkeeper wasn't really on the ball. There were loads of mistakes; some bills were paid twice and others not at all, there was missing data, and data incorrectly reconciled. It was a disaster. So, I made a bold choice: I once again took over the bookkeeping. I thought: How hard could it be to pay the bills, reconcile the cloud accounting software and submit the Business Activity Statement?

For international readers, the Business Activity Statement, or BAS return as it's more commonly known, is a compliance requirement for some Australian businesses.

This time I'd apply myself. I'd read everything I needed to read and make sure I did it all properly. I'd be fine and see my accountant at the end of the financial year.

While I didn't magically become gifted at bookkeeping overnight – I still didn't do numbers – what I did do was consistency and attention to detail. So, as the newly appointed numbers gal, I spent a lot of time on the bookkeeping (too much time if I'm frank), and that gave me confidence that I was doing what was needed and doing it well.

About 18 months later, we were at the end of our second tax year in business. We'd made a small profit, and at the time, I remember feeling pretty smug about business.

I mean, here I was, this girl who didn't do numbers, and I was looking after the finances! I had to learn bookkeeping and prepare BAS returns, and I was *nailing it*.

So, you can imagine the shock I felt on that fateful day in September 2003, when the email popped into my inbox from my accountant telling me we owed the tax office money.

And not just a small amount of money – a huge sum.

$42,000.

Initially, I was in disbelief. I remember calling my accountant and asking if they could explain how we accrued such a massive tax debt. Keep in mind this was 20 years ago – I used an inflation calculator online and it confirmed this would be like getting a surprise debt of $70,000 today.

I'd been so careful about the finances, and even I knew enough to know that there couldn't be $42,000 in tax to pay on the small profit we'd made. So how had things gone so wrong?

I couldn't get my head around the debt and naturally, at that time I blamed myself. The debt was all my fault. It was because I didn't do numbers. I was too cheap to pay someone really good to help and I didn't understand it enough and look at the mess I made.

My accountant explained it to me, but it still didn't make much sense. She was an educated professional and I was not, so what they'd said had to be right, I decided – I just needed to accept the debt and move on.

The problem was that we didn't have a cent in savings in our business.

And at the time, with four small kids, we didn't have savings, full stop.

So, I told my accountant we couldn't afford to pay the $42,000 by the deadline as we didn't have the money set aside, and we would need to pay it off. I remember the shame I felt and the lecture I received from the accountant about how foolish we were for not having set aside money to pay for our taxes, and for not having anticipated the tax expense. But honestly, with my absolute lack of financial knowledge, how would I have expected such a considerable debt?

At that moment, I realised that despite feeling in control, I was financially illiterate. I knew nothing about the financial side of the business, and worse, I didn't know who to reach out to for help.

To add insult to injury, my accountant informed me that because we had entered into a payment arrangement with the tax office, we'd essentially landed on the ATO's naughty list. It meant that until the debt was paid off, each and every time we submitted a quarterly Business Activity Statement or any other tax compliance, we were liable to pay our tax obligations in full - no more payment arrangements or extended due dates on offer!

As luck would have it, another BAS period ended two weeks later, and we owed a considerable amount of money on that return too. Because all of the money we'd saved for our BAS had gone as a deposit on the $42,000 debt we owed, we couldn't afford to pay our BAS either and had to add this new amount to our overall debt. We were in a world of pain!

Just what every new business needs: the giant burden of debt

If you've ever had money problems in your business or life, you understand the stress that a large debt brings. And when the debt comes with hard deadlines, the stress goes to a whole new level.

In my case, having debt, particularly one you feel directly responsible for, impacts everything, from how you spend your money to your relationship and how you look at yourself.

As an adult, I believed I should have had a handle on this stuff. You might be able to relate to this feeling? I wasn't supposed to start a business and put our family into debt. Our business was our family's only source of income, and the intention was to create financial freedom, not financial ruin!

Now, we were trying to keep that business afloat and service an almost impossible amount of debt, too.

I couldn't believe someone as smart as me could have landed our family in such a precarious position. I was in charge of the finances and failed. Though my husband didn't actually come out and say it, I'm sure he felt the same way.

I'm not over-stating it when I say: that tax office debt and the stress it brought on our family and the business, took me to the edge of my sanity. I can't tell you how many sleepless nights I had, how much I doubted myself and every decision I made going forward, and how every day became a bigger pity party.

I was drowning in self-doubt, shame, and the inability to forgive myself for the catastrophic mistake I'd made, one that had put my family and my business in so much jeopardy.

My husband and I talked about how we could change things. We couldn't sell the toy shop at that stage because it wasn't profitable enough. If one of us went out and got a job we'd struggle because we had four kids and no childcare. We had a full-time store to manage but couldn't afford to pay a full-time staff member. We felt utterly stuck in our business and our debt, and none of that eased the shame and embarrassment I felt every day.

The day we opened our first store, our friends quietly commented how we would fail; at the time, half of *all* small businesses failed in the first five years, and now we were fulfilling that prophecy. It was a dark and terrible time in my life.

But I was born with a strong resilience muscle; there's no doubt about it. And after a few weeks of wallowing, it was time for my pity party to end. I needed a new plan, a new way forward.

I'd grown up in a house where money was in short supply and that feeling of lack and insecurity was still very much my money story. Plus, numbers had never been my strength. But at that moment I decided I needed a new money story and some education. I had to become financially literate to stay in business and so I set about writing a new plan that spoke to my definition of success.

Step one was to find a new accountant, and 12 months later, I hired someone incredible. My new accountant did some digging and could share with me why the business had accrued a $42,000 tax debt and why it was, in fact, an accounting mistake – but not an accounting mistake that I'd made, an accounting mistake the former accountant had made.

The mistake was simple: accounting 101, you could say, and one that our former accountant should never have made.

In Australia, when you register for an Australian Business Number and set up your business, you must decide how to report on your business tax return and quarterly Business Activity Statement. You have two choices, either Cash Basis or Accrual Basis. You see, accounting is a date-driven system, and each type of accounting, cash and accrual, has a different treatment of dates and how you accrue tax as a result.

I'll explain a little more about cash and accrual accounting later on in the book because, in reality, most people don't know how they've registered and don't understand the difference. As we found out, though, it's essential to know how, at the very least, your business has chosen to register and to let your tax professional know. We had registered using the cash basis, but our former accountant had been processing returns using the accruals basis. And what an impact that error had made.

While there was nothing we could do about a retrospective debt, at that moment, when my new accountant explained the error, I was given an enormous gift: freedom. He'd taken time to explain to me what had gone wrong. And, while ultimately, we may have been liable for the $42K in tax down the track, I felt relief in knowing that the error wasn't my fault.

Despite that disappointment, his explanation freed me from my guilt. It allowed me to breathe again and finally begin to build the confidence I'd lost. Plus, now I knew what to look for at tax time, so no matter who did our taxes going forward, I would never allow that kind of mistake again in my business.

Believe it or not, it took that conversation with my new accountant for the lightbulb to finally go off and help me realise what I needed to do next.

I had to get educated and increase my financial literacy, in order to go forward confidently and create the sustainable and thriving business I desired.

And I needed to learn as much as possible about business finances, because I knew there was power in that knowledge and education.

No half measures here!

I finally understood that increasing my financial business knowledge could be the key to unlocking all the other parts of the business and turning it from one burgeoning under debt back into a healthy business. Knowing there was light at the end of the tunnel, that there was hope for my business, and that the key to unlocking the potential in my business was as simple as increasing my financial knowledge was a game-changer.

The next logical thing to do was work out how I could learn about the financial side of business.

However, I would not suggest you do what I did next.

It's only now that I can admit it was a little extreme in my approach. I didn't just learn the basics ... I went all in. I decided to become a Registered BAS agent!

To achieve that goal, I had to do an accounting course and verbal exams and undertake 1,000 hours of supervised BAS return preparation over the course of 18 months in an accounting firm. No half measures here!

By then, we had two retail stores and an e-commerce business. I was studying, raising our four children who were all under 10 and I was working full time in an accounting firm specialising in insolvency.

Although I was busy (the world's greatest understatement?!), the knowledge I gained, particularly while working in insolvency, increased my understanding of my business and inspired me to continue.

During that time, I learned to spot the red flags in the businesses I worked with and how to turn a loss-making business into one that was profitable. I understood how to decipher financial reports and pick up errors.

But that time also taught me that the numbers in a business tell a story, and that story could help turn a floundering business into a thriving business with just a few minor tweaks.

It taught me that building firm financial foundations in any business was the cornerstone of creating a successful, profitable, sustainable business. My money mindset also improved exponentially because now I felt like I had the key to unlock the magic!

That shift was the beginning of my journey into financial education for other business owners. My knowledge and the experience I'd gained allowed me to improve my business and help other business owners, too.

We'd both grown tired of retail, so, in 2017 we closed our stores, said goodbye to the world of toys (and to tax debt), my hubby returned to full-time work, and I started a business offering bookkeeping and compliance services. Imagine that – me, still not a numbers person, willingly deciding to throw myself headfirst into a career rooted in numbers!

Over the next five and a half years, I built a business with multiple income streams, worked with incredible, creative women in business, as well as a few good men, and helped them increase their financial knowledge and create profitable businesses they loved.

Thanks to that $42,000 tax debt, I had transformed my own financial literacy, and as a result I now had a business I loved, one built on numbers. For a girl who didn't do numbers just a few years earlier, it was an incredible achievement.

As it turned out, it was only the beginning.

In February 2023, I sold off the bookkeeping and compliance part of my business for a profit. A profit that allowed me the freedom to pursue a bigger mission; helping other business owners increase their financial literacy, pursue financial freedom and achieve success. And, because my business had multiple income streams, one which focused on financial education, it meant I wasn't starting again from scratch.

So, as I go into this legacy phase of business, I aim to work with as many business owners as possible, providing them with the tools and good money habits required to achieve success, whatever that means to them in this season of life and business.

That's why I wrote this book. Because when you put aside the complicated jargon, those annoying spreadsheets and the endless reports, making money in business can be simple. It's not just a matter of making more than you spend but setting your business up to weather the inevitable storms coming your way.

Like it or not, understanding the business numbers is essential to business success because the numbers can unlock everything you need to build a profitable and sustainable business.

And no matter who you are or what you do, as a business owner, you must understand the money. Full stop.

Right now, financial literacy is more important than ever, especially for women and young people. But, by acquiring some basic knowledge and skills, I know it's possible to improve the statistics. And while this book is specifically for business, you'll find a number of the concepts here can equally apply to your personal finances too.

I hope this book will help you drastically improve your business and life. Cherry-pick what you need and come back to it over and over again.

My tip is to habit stack, employ one thing today, get it working and then come back and introduce the next concept.

And if you find yourself doubting if this is for you or if you're even capable of improving the financial side of your business, take a minute to remember that girl who, back in 2002, didn't do numbers and landed in a world of pain with enormous tax debt ... but who came out the other side, sold a business and now has the luxury of choosing her next adventure.

You're not alone because if I can do this, so can you!

MONEY MAGNET TIP:

Movement creates movement, so take a leap of faith, make a commitment to change just one thing today and watch everything around you start to change too.

How to use this book

This book has been designed as a practical tool for your business, no matter what stage of business you're at. You can consume the book from cover to cover or go directly to the chapter that will help you and your business the most right now.

Throughout each chapter, I've used case studies based on real-life examples (I've changed names and business types for privacy) to help illustrate strategies you can implement to benefit your business.

In addition, each chapter contains activities, actions and prompts to help you determine where you're at now and the next steps needed to achieve your goal. There are links to an external website where you can download templates and other tools to help you improve your financial foundations, set good habits and build a business that fits your definition of success.

Understanding business finance should be something everyone has access to, so no matter how you learn, there is something in this book for you.

Enjoy!

Let's get started:

Get clear on the problem you're trying to solve so you can work through the solution.

What inspired you to buy this book?

Was it the idea of increasing your financial knowledge?

Are you in a world of financial pain with your business?

Perhaps you're also in tax debt, or maybe you're not paying yourself a wage and super, but you'd very much like to?

It could be the case that your money mindset needs a shakeup, or it's time to get the pricing right in your business.

You might have a single reason, or it could be a combination of the above. Whatever your reason or reasons, I'd love you to grab a journal and start writing.

Why?

Because when we set an intention and get crystal clear or verbalise our reason for doing something, we're more likely to work towards that goal and achieve it.

I also think it's essential to go on record and understand where you're at right now, your starting point, because when you look back – a few weeks or a few months from now – you'll see how far you've come, and that will empower you to continue. And I'm all about empowerment; it's one of my personal values and my brand values, too.

Journal prompts:

1. What inspired you to buy this book?

2. What's the most significant business problem you're trying to solve?

3. What do you want to achieve when you've done the work?

Where are you at right now?

On a scale of 1 to 10, 1 being **'In the dark or very concerned'** and 10 being **'Super Savvy - You've got this!'** answer the following:

1. Where would you put your financial literacy right now?

2. How do you feel about the financial side of your business today – is it working well or is it time to get some help?

3. As you look into the future, how do you feel about your business and the economic outlook over the next 12 months?

4. Do you know what success means to you and do you have a clear pathway to success mapped out?

5. Do you have great business money habits in place?

6. Do you know what it costs you to run your business each month and year?

7. How do you feel about your pricing – is it working in your favour and driving profits for you, or does it need some work?

8. Where is your business mindset at right now? Are money blocks or a negative mindset getting in your way? For example: Perhaps you're in the habit of regularly making poor choices with money and then feeling guilt and shame.

9. When you think about your customer base are you concerned or confident?

10. Finally, how healthy is your business emergency savings fund?

Glossary of Terms & Other Definitions

There are lots of business finance terms you should be aware of as a business owner. Understanding some of these terms and concepts will help you communicate with the experts who assist you in your business and become better equipped to make informed decisions.

While normally, a glossary would appear at the back of a book, I felt it important to explain these terms upfront, to allow you to make more immediate sense of the chapters to follow.

Hint: you might like to refer to this section as you work through the chapters.

Business Money Lingo

Assets: Anything a business owns that has value, such as property, inventory, or equipment.

Asset register: Just as it sounds, this is a list of assets owned by the business, those physical resources that could be sold in the event of the business closing down. From the computer and phone you use to your office furniture and equipment, large machinery and items you purchase for your staff to use, an asset register is useful for keeping track of business assets and their worth for taxation, statutory and sale-of-business purposes.

You can also use your asset register to keep track of serial numbers, item make and model numbers and warranty information. It's best to record each asset separately and to add to your asset register as you purchase any new equipment.

Balance sheet: A financial statement that provides a snapshot of a business's financial position at a specific time. It shows a business's assets, liabilities, and equity. For more information about the Balance sheet see chapter 8.

Break-even point: The point at which a business's revenue equals its expenses, resulting in zero profit or loss.

Budget: A plan that outlines a business's expected income and expenses for a specific period. For more information about budgeting see chapter 9.

Budgeting: The process of creating a plan for allocating a business's resources, such as money, time and personnel, so that the business can achieve its goals. Budgeting can involve setting revenue, expenses, and profit targets and tracking actual performance against those targets. For more information about budgeting, see chapter 9.

Business turnover: Refers to the total revenue a business generates from its operations over a specific period, typically a year. Calculate turnover by adding all the sales revenue the business earns from its products or services during a particular period.

Capital: The money or assets a business uses to fund its operations; think money in the bank or savings.

Cash flow: The amount of cash coming into and going out of a business. Positive cash flow means the business has more money coming in than going out; negative cash flow means the opposite. For more information about cash flow, see chapter 10.

Cost of goods sold (COGS): Refers to the direct costs of producing or manufacturing a product or service. COGS includes materials, labour, and other expenses directly related to the production process.

For example: If a bakery sells a cake, the COGS would include the cost of the ingredients used to make the cake, the wages paid to the baker and any assistants involved in making the cake, and any other costs directly related to producing the cake, such as packaging materials or fuel for delivery.

Depreciation: The decrease in the value of an asset over time due to wear and tear. There's a specific set of guidelines for depreciating an asset, so it's best to speak to your financial professional, who can guide you on the depreciation calculation.

Equity: The value of a business's assets minus its liabilities. Equity is what the business is worth on paper. If you ever want to sell your business, the equity number can help work out how much the business is worth.

Expenses: The costs incurred by a business to operate, such as rent, salaries, and materials, to name a few.

Gross profit: The revenue a business earns minus the cost of goods sold (COGS). Gross profit is the profit before deducting operating expenses.

The gross profit figure helps to determine how much money is left over after the direct costs of producing the product or service are paid for and helps business owners budget for operating expenses.

Investment planning: The process of creating a plan for investing a business's resources, such as money and other assets, to achieve its financial goals. Investment planning can involve choosing appropriate investments for the business's risk tolerance, time horizon, and other factors.

Liabilities: Debts or financial obligations a business owes to others, such as loans or unpaid bills. Liabilities can also include taxes and unpaid wages and employee benefits.

Loss: When expenses are greater than revenue, and the business is losing money, the business is operating at a loss.

Net profit: Is a business's revenue minus all its expenses (including COGS plus operating costs). The amount left is called the net profit. Net profit is a key number in your business and can be tailored to your business goals.

Operating expenses: Also known as overheads, refer to the costs incurred by a business. These costs are not directly related to the production or manufacture of a product or service but are necessary for running the business.

Examples of expenses or overheads may include:

- Rent or lease payments for office space or equipment.

- Utilities such as electricity, water, and internet.

- Salaries or wages for employees who are not directly involved in production, such as administrative staff or salespeople.

- Marketing and advertising expenses.

- Insurance premiums.

- Legal or accounting fees.

- Office supplies.

- Subscription fees.

- Training or skills development costs.

- Travel and car costs, for example.

Expenses or overheads are typically recurring costs that a business incurs regularly. Tracking expenses helps manage cash flow and optimise profitability. A business can reduce its overall costs and increase its profit margin by monitoring and controlling operating expenses.

Profit: The difference between revenue and expenses is called profit. If revenue is greater than expenses, the business is making a profit.

Profit and Loss statement (P&L): A financial statement that shows a business's revenue, expenses, and profit or loss over a specific period, such as a month, quarter, or year. For more information about P&L statements see chapter 8.

Profit margin: Think of profit margin as a way to measure how much money you make from your business activities. It's like asking, 'How much profit am I making for every dollar of sales I make?'

For example: Let's say you sell handmade jewellery and make $10,000 in revenue from your monthly sales. However, expenses such as buying materials, paying for website hosting, and hiring a part-time assistant cost you $8,000. In this case, your monthly net income (profit) is $2,000 ($10,000 - $8,000).

To calculate your profit margin, divide your net income by your total revenue. In this case, your profit margin would be 20% ($2,000 / $10,000).

So, what does this 20% profit margin mean? It means that for every dollar you make in sales, you can keep 20 cents as profit. Your profit margin can help you evaluate the efficiency of your product or services and your business. Understanding your profitability can also help you identify areas to improve your business.

A higher profit margin is obviously better because it means you are keeping more of your sales revenue as profit. However, it's essential to consider your industry and the competitive landscape when evaluating your profit margin. A lower profit margin may be acceptable if it is typical for your industry. But you should always aim to improve your profitability where possible.

Record keeping: The process of keeping accurate and detailed records of a business's financial transactions, such as income, expenses, staffing and investments. Record keeping is essential for monitoring the financial health of the business, as well as for tax purposes. For more information about record keeping see chapter 11.

Revenue: The income a business generates from selling its products or services.

ROI (Return on Investment): A measure of how much profit a business makes in relation to the amount of money it has invested.

Tax obligations: The legal requirements for a business to pay taxes to the Government. Tax obligations can include income tax, payroll tax, sales tax, and other types of taxes. For more information about compliance see chapter 11.

Tax planning: Involves managing a business's finances and minimising its tax liability. Tax planning can involve taking advantage of tax deductions, credits, and exemptions and using tax-advantaged investment strategies. Your financial advisor is best positioned to assist with tax planning as they know your state or territory's legislation, tax obligations and requirements.

Cash vs Accrual Accounting

Before we wrap up all the key terms, cash and accrual accounting are worth mentioning. This one concept was the basis of my massive tax debt, shared in chapter one. When you registered your business, you might have been asked whether you'd like to register as a cash or accrual business, or your accountant or financial professional may have chosen for you when preparing your first business return. In some countries, you may have no choice. When you set up a cloud accounting system, it's a question you need to be able to answer, so it's essential to understand the different methods.

Why? Because the answer to that question will determine your business tax future; it will determine how your taxes are calculated and filed and how your compliance is calculated, filed and paid.

In a nutshell, accounting is a date-driven system, so everything is in the timing. When you reconcile day-to-day transactions, create invoices or enter bills, the one thing you always do is enter a date. Whether you process accounts using a ledger, a spreadsheet or a cloud accounting system, it all comes down to the date.

Cash-based accounting recognises revenue and expenses on the date the money is received or paid out of the business account. Most small businesses tend to use the cash-based method. It makes sense because it can aid in preserving cash flow, for example, as the business will only be required to pay tax on the money once it's received. Likewise, you won't get any tax deduction benefit on expenses until your bills have been paid.

On the other hand, **Accrual-based accounting** is generally used by big businesses. It recognises revenue and expenses using the date that appears on the invoice or bill. You may or may not have received the income; you may or may not have paid the bill, but for the purposes of the accrual accounts, the revenue is recognised regardless of whether it's in the bank or not, and the expenses are recognised irrespective of whether the bill has been paid.

If you want to learn more about cash or accrual accounting or would like to know what method your business uses, talk to your accountant or your local tax office. Ensure this is reflected in your cloud accounting system, if you use one, or when you process your compliance or tax returns, especially if you do them yourself.

Ascension Model / Value Ladders

These are not accounting terms but it's worth adding here because no matter what sort of business you have, chances are you'll have a number of products or services on offer for your ideal client.

From the least expensive to the most expensive, your ascension model or value ladder is simply the suite of options on offer so that your ideal client has the opportunity to work with you at different levels of value and service. While both of these terms refer to similar concepts, there are some subtle differences between the two.

A **value ladder** is a framework that outlines the different levels of value that a business can offer to its customers, think of it as the journey a customer might take from your lowest ticket item all the way up to your most expensive or VIP offer.

Typically, each level of the value ladder offers more value or benefits to your ideal client, as well as a higher price tag than the offer before it. The purpose of a value ladder is to provide a clear path for customers to follow, one that will increase their engagement with the business and encourage their loyalty.

An example of a Value Ladder:

1. Level 1: Basic Product – An entry-level product that offers essen-

tial features and functionality at an affordable price.

2. Level 2: Standard Product – A mid-level product with additional features and functionality that offers more value to customers.

3. Level 3: Premium Product – A high-end product that offers the best features and functionality, as well as exclusive benefits like customer support, warranties, or extended service plans.

4. Level 4: Deluxe Product – A premium, customised product that offers a unique and personalised experience, with additional features, accessories, or customization options that are tailored to the customer's needs.

5. Level 5: Bundle Offer – Offering a bundle of products that provides additional value and savings compared to buying each product individually.

6. Level 6: Subscription Service – Offering a subscription service that provides ongoing access to exclusive products, discounts, and other benefits.

Example of a Value Ladder – Service based interior design business:

1. Level 1: Design Consultation – A one-hour consultation for a fixed fee to discuss design ideas and recommendations.

2. Level 2: Room Design Plan – A comprehensive design plan for one room including colour scheme, furniture recommendations, and decor ideas.

3. Level 3: Full Home Design – A complete design plan for an entire home or apartment, including detailed floor plans, furniture, and decor recommendations.

4. Level 4: Premium Design Services – A fully customised and bespoke design service, including project management and exclu-

sive access to top-of-the-line furniture and decor.

Your clients could enter your business at any point along the value ladder journey and while they may stay around for the entire trip, these customers will often enter your business for a specific service, a one and done and then be on their way.

An **ascension model**, on the other hand, is a strategy that focuses on nurturing existing customers and encouraging them to move up the ladder of value within the business. The idea behind an ascension model is that it's more cost-effective to retain existing customers than to acquire new ones, so the focus is on creating a great customer experience and offering additional value to keep customers engaged and loyal. This can include offering personalised recommendations, exclusive content or access, and other perks or benefits that incentivise customers to continue investing in the business.

So, kind of same same but with subtle differences; think of a value ladder as a journey offering different price points to customers, they could buy into the journey at any point, whereas, an ascension model is more strategic, a tool to encourage customers to enter your ecosystem and stay around for the entire trip.

Example of an Ascension Model:

1. Level 1: Free Trial, Free product sample or a discount code – Offering a free trial or demo of the product to introduce potential customers to its features and benefits.

2. Level 2: Starter Kit – Offering a starter kit that includes a selection of products that provide a complete user experience and encourage customers to invest in additional products.

3. Level 3: Basic Plan – Offering a low-cost, full size, entry-level product or plan that provides basic features and functionality to

customers who want to try the product before committing to a higher-priced plan.

4. Level 4: Premium Plan – Offering a premium plan that includes more advanced features and functionality, as well as additional benefits like priority customer support, discounts on future purchases, or exclusive content.

5. Level 5: VIP Plan – Offering a VIP plan that includes all of the features and benefits of the premium plan, as well as exclusive access to new products, early access to sales, and other perks that are not available to lower-tier customers.

Example of an Ascension Model – Service based interior design business:

1. Level 1: Free Design Resource – A lead magnet offering a free design resource such as a how-to or downloadable guide or checklist to attract potential customers and showcase your expertise.

2. Level 2: Design Inspiration Package – Offering a package of curated design inspiration images, along with a personalised mood board and a one-hour consultation to discuss ideas and recommendations.

3. Level 3: Full Home Design Plan – Offering a complete design plan for an entire home or apartment, including detailed floor plans, furniture, and decor recommendations, and project management services.

4. Level 4: VIP Design Services – Offering a bespoke, VIP design experience that includes unlimited consultations, exclusive access to top-of-the-line furniture and decor, and a dedicated design team.

In this ascension model example, each level offers a different level of customisation and personalisation as the customer moves up the ladder. The focus is on gradually nurturing potential customers and encouraging them to invest in more comprehensive design services as they build trust in the designer's expertise and value.

Mindset

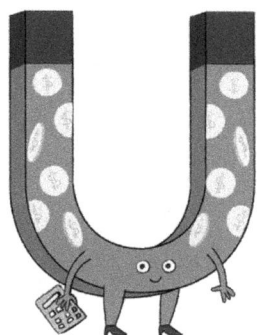

Chapter 2

Setting the Stage for Success

'Energy is the essence of life. Every day, you decide how you're going to use it by knowing what you want and what it takes to reach that goal and by maintaining focus.'

Oprah Winfrey

When it comes to business and life, I always look through the glass-half-full lens, taking a proactive approach and believing that anything is possible. But I'm also a realist. After 30 years in business, I know that life and business are a bit like a roller-coaster; there'll be lots of ups and downs. But there'll also be different seasons: the figurative winter when nothing seems to go your way, and you want to curl up in a ball and forget the world exists, to the beautiful spring and summer when abundance is all around, and life (and business) is one giant celebration.

Honestly, it's not what I expected when I started in business and sometimes, that unpredictability is enough to make you want to walk away altogether.

Over the years, I've been on a wild ride and experienced lots of highs and lows. Along the way, I learned a trick that helped me thrive. It's all about creating expectations and that starts with understanding your definition of success and what it means to you in this current season of life and business. It's why, now, I'm all about setting the stage for success and understanding what it means to me as I navigate the road ahead.

So, my definition of success is something I work on every quarter – yep, that's right. It changes constantly! When I begin working with a new client, it's one of the first questions I ask them. Why? Because your business and your business goals will change and grow often. What's important right now might be less critical in six or twelve months. And when life happens, as it invariably will, you should have the luxury of adapting your business success goals to fit in around your life while still making money in the process.

So, in this chapter, we will set the stage for success. We'll explore success, why it matters, what it means to you, and how you'll celebrate when you achieve each milestone.

What is success and why does it matter?

We hear a lot about success. What it takes to run a successful business, and what you need to have a successful life, and most of us want the proverbial key to success: the secret that will help us achieve our heart's desire. I was so curious to learn the secrets of a successful business that I started a podcast on the topic, interviewing 'successful' entrepreneurs who seem to have achieved that elusive dream.

But here's the thing: when you start a business, while you usually have an idea of what success will look like for you, it's so often built on perception – something you've seen someone else achieve or what the person over there seems to be doing. It's rarely a fully formed, unique idea of what your success end game will look like. Even if it is, I guarantee that after a few rough months in business, you'll either forget that end goal altogether or realise it needs to drastically change.

So often, thinking about success is a one-and-done. However, under-standing what success means to you and more importantly, regularly redefining that success goal, IS one of the main secrets to creating a successful business.

Bottom line: while the dictionary defines success as achieving an out-come or goal, for me, business success is more about remembering why you started your business, acknowledging what's going on in your life at any given moment and then setting realistic, manageable goals that are unique to your situation and make sense in the season of life you find yourself in now.

If you can do that often, you'll not only be able to adjust as you go, but you're less likely to feel like a 'failure' even when you don't tick off all your goals.

Understanding what success means for you can be a driving force for growth both in your business and your life. It will give you direction, help you stay accountable, be more motivated and confident in your decisions, and adapt and evolve as needed.

What does success mean for you in this season of life and business?

Note that I asked what it means for YOU.

Not for your partner, your family, neighbours, friends or that influencer or business owner you follow on social media, but *you*.

I'm talking about the life and business you'd conjure up if you had a magic wand or were granted three wishes. It's the idea that lives in your heart of hearts, one that you're sure you'd achieve if only …

And ... yep, that's about the time reality steps in, or worse, your inner antagonist takes over. You're back in a world of negativity and comparison, and the road ahead seems impossible to navigate.

This is especially true when it comes to the financial side of business. When we think about business success, more often than not, we equate that success with making money, lots and lots of money, because that's what we've been conditioned to believe and what everyone else seems capable of doing.

And while I'm all for creating a profitable business, I want to tell you a secret. I've seen behind the curtain on those so-called high six and seven-figure businesses. While they're genuinely bringing in those high revenue numbers, their profit – what's left over when all the bills are paid – is often not what you'd expect.

So many of us get caught up in what our business success *should* look like. Is it the five-figure months or the six or seven-figure years? Is it a number on a profit and loss statement, or the dollars in the bank?

But success can and should look different for everyone because, at the heart of it, no two businesses are the same. Businesses are run by people, and because we're all different, it should be personal when we think of business success.

As you set the stage for your success, I want you to put yourself in a bubble, look inward, and think about what success means for you right now, especially in terms of money.

When you think about success and what it means for you, remember to take a moment and make a conscious decision about what you want your business to look like; what you might achieve if you knew you couldn't fail.

More importantly, think about where your business intersects with your stage of life and if, in the season you're in right now, you might need to temper the expectations you place on yourself.

As a business owner, you are what makes your business unique. Therefore, it's essential to understand what success means to you and your business. While your success goal can look like someone else's, they will not be the same. Why? Because you're you; it's that simple.

Remember that success isn't always about the business turnover or the money in the bank; it doesn't have to be about your numbers on social media, your mailing list or how many people turned up for your webinar.

It could be as simple as the number of hours you want to work every week, getting to spend time with your kids and taking them to their after-school activities, or it could be about buying yourself a new car, or giving the keynote at your favourite conference.

Whatever it is, one thing I know for sure about your definition of success is that it can and will change regularly, so make sure it's something you revisit often, particularly as your business landscape changes.

When I started my first business back in 1994, I had a newborn, so success for me was ticking off the list of phone calls I had to make, with no crying baby in the background, and completing the tasks I needed to perform each week to keep the publishing process going. Often, it meant grabbing a work hour here or there in between feeds and sleep, but it worked and that was ok.

Once the kids were at school, I thought success would be getting all the household chores done and giving a solid 4-5 hours to the retail stores each weekday and all during school hours – boy, was I wrong! There was no way I managed to get all of that done! I wanted to be around for school events and have the flexibility to support the boys with their sport, so my idea of success needed a radical change. So, I modified my expectations, outsourced a little more and accepted that some nights, when the kids went to bed, I needed to work on the business.

When the kids were in high school life, success was different again. Although there weren't as many school events to attend and certainly little need for me to help with the homework, two of my boys were elite athletes so there were lots of hours of driving to and from training, and I needed to manage that alongside my business. Success at that time meant not allowing myself to be an overachiever and not feeling guilty every five minutes for what I *didn't* manage to get done.

Now, in the legacy phase of business, and with a smaller operation to manage, success to me is tied to outcome – what I can do to help other business owners get to where they want to go. So, I measure my success based on what my clients achieve. And while that may sound a little cheesy, I wouldn't have it any other way.

As you read through the crib notes of my success journey over the years, you might be wondering why I haven't mentioned money or reaching a turnover total or profit number as my measure of success. It's simple really. I started my business journey to spend time with my family and for the freedom my own business might offer.

For that reason, I made a decision early on that I didn't want to be a slave to the dollars and would never tie my success to money. As long as my business was profitable, I earned a wage and I could spend time with my kids, that was all that mattered.

> **MONEY MAGNET TIP:**
>
> Remember, success is as individual as you are, and you get to decide what it means to you now and in the future. So, if you're not sure what your success means to you right now, grab a notebook or journal and imagine your dream life. What would you do if you knew you couldn't fail?
>
> No matter how outrageous you believe your answer is in the moment, take time and then work backwards from your dream outcome to where you are today. What steps do you need to take to get to where you want to go?

How will you celebrate?

Just as achieving success and reaching your business goals is important, so is celebrating.

So many of us gloss over life's milestones as we rush towards the next milestone. As business owners, we're often so caught up in the busyness of business that we gloss over a win and simply move on to the next thing on the list.

I get it – I'm guilty of it, too. But celebrating matters, because it sends a message to yourself and your team that you did something fantastic, ticked something off the list, and achieved a milestone, no matter how small. In celebrating your win, you're acknowledging your success. Those good endorphins will motivate you to continue working towards the next thing.

Plus, we're happy to celebrate for other people so why not celebrate you, too! And that goes double for the smaller wins!

So, how will you celebrate your next success?

MONEY MAGNET TIP:

When you achieve your goals, how will you celebrate? Your 'reward' doesn't need to cost a fortune; it could be something that doesn't have any financial value at all, as simple as a morning off from work to have a swim in the ocean, a coffee date with your bestie or even a dance party in your living room with your favourite takeaway meal.

Celebrating in action – Rebecca Saunders

My lovely friend Rebecca Saunders, founder of The Champagne Lounge, has made a business out of celebrating other businesswomen, especially those living and working in regional and remote areas across Australia.

Rebecca has always had a philosophy of celebration in her business journey. In a previous life, she owned a multi-million-dollar revenue-generating video production business – one where she hit big goals often – and because she started from scratch with very little money to back her journey, hitting her milestones was crucial.

For Rebecca, nothing equals celebration more than a bottle of good bubbly. So, at the start of each year, Rebecca buys six bottles of her favourite French champagne, puts them in the fridge and adds a post-it note to the outside of each box highlighting a big goal. When that goal is achieved, Rebecca gets to pop that bottle of champagne and celebrate.

Setting realistic as well as unrealistic goals has motivated Rebecca to stay mindful of the end game and keep striving, even in the tough times. As she always says, 'Seeing those champagne bottles every time I open the fridge keeps my goals front of mind'. Rebecca credits this annual habit as one of the keys to helping her achieve both business and life success.

In her business The Champagne Lounge, Rebecca still performs this annual ritual. And today, hitting those small goals is just as important as the champagne celebration when the big wins roll around.

Rebecca's advice: 'Always have a mindset that anything is possible. Gamify your business success by first visualising yourself achieving your goals, both the big and the small, then believing and watching it happen.'

Rebecca also points out that you don't need to spend a lot of money on champagne to celebrate your wins. Instead, choose a reward that's meaningful to you, an afternoon off, a day at the beach, an indulgent afternoon at the spa and use that for motivation. The key is to not just write your goals in a book and forget them; they need to be front and centre so you can see them daily and stay focused.

Put it into practice:

Let's clarify your definition of success and why it matters to you. Grab a journal and answer these questions as you review the way forward. Remember that you don't need to do this for a specific period; you might choose a month, three months, a year or five years. The important thing is to focus on the bigger question, and that is: *'What does success mean to you in this season of life and business?'*

What season of life and business are you in right now?

- Take a moment to think about where you are right now, in your personal life, relationships, lifestyle, family situation and business. Do you have life responsibilities that might impact your business? For example, you need to take care of kids and do the school run or care for elderly parents or you have fur babies who need extra attention.

- What stage of business are you in? A start-up, two years in or more established? A growth stage, have you plateaued, or are you winding back, perhaps in a legacy phase?

- Are you energised about your business or in need of a business break?

There are no right or wrong answers here. The focus is to get honest with where you are and what you can and cannot take on. We'd all like to be superheroes and work at 110 percent all the time, but sometimes it's just impossible.

When you think about the road ahead, what does success look like for you in this season of life and business?

Next, it's time to set your intention for this next period in your business.

Need some inspiration for your next success goal? Here are some ideas:

- Set aside time each week to work ON your business instead of IN your business. Why not spend an hour and do a Money Monday or Finance Friday?

- Start paying yourself a regular weekly wage and superannuation, too. If you can't afford to do this – something needs to change.

- Streamline your workflow with better systems and processes. Everything, even the smallest and simplest part of your business, can benefit from a clear system.

- Hire a virtual assistant.

- Work only between 9am and 3pm.

- Bank account looks a little sad - maybe success means improving business cash flow. Look at increasing prices or savings on your expenses as a starting point.

- Plan a holiday and to get really excited about it, make a booking.

- Review the services you offer and your current pricing. Is it time to increase prices? Hint: if you can't afford to pay yourself a wage, or you haven't increased your prices in a couple of years, the answer is probably yes.

In the final part of the exercise, it's important to get clear about intention, so ask yourself:

Why is it essential that you achieve success now? Why does success matter to you?

For example: Achieving success makes you feel good about yourself, your business and your life. And feeling good is the fuel you need to keep moving forward.

What do you need to do to achieve your goal? What's the one big thing that comes to mind?

There's no success without action, so this prompt is simple. What is it that you need to do to achieve your goal?

For example: If earning $120K in revenue in the next twelve months will make you feel like a success, what do you need to do to achieve that revenue? It might be increasing your prices or streamlining or automating a service you currently offer so you can reach more clients.

How will you know you've succeeded? What measurement will you put in place?

No one will be tapping you on the shoulder and congratulating you on your new success, so how will you know when you've succeeded?

For example: Do you need to put a date in the diary to review your progress or create a visible reminder like a vision board? Can you rope in a business bestie to keep you accountable?

How will you celebrate?

You know I want you to celebrate, so decide now precisely how you'll celebrate your win, no matter how big or small it is.

Chapter 3

How to Overcome Limiting Beliefs and Money Setbacks

'My dad had a Rolls Royce.'

Victoria Beckham

In the 2023 documentary *Beckham*, Victoria Beckham was grilled about her upbringing. She initially shared with viewers that she was from a middle-class background. But Victoria's husband, David, was having none of it and quickly called her out with a simple question: *'What sort of car did your Dad use to drive you to school?'*

After a few awkward moments and attempts at an answer, Victoria finally uttered the now infamous line, *'My dad had a Rolls Royce'*. It was enlightening to see that even someone who is so clearly *not* middle class felt the need to justify where her journey started. It seems even Victoria Beckham has a money story and money mindset she can't shake.

Just like Posh, we've all got a money story and a set of beliefs that shape our thoughts about money and how we see the world and ourselves, aka our mindset.

Those beliefs and the values we hold influence our decision-making, how we think and act in our day-to-day life and, in turn, how we feel about ourselves, our money and whether we're winning at life or failing spectacularly.

Most of us don't think about our mindset. It's not a conscious participant in our daily lives but rather there in the background, subconsciously informing the choices we make.

According to Stanford psychologist Carol Dweck, our mindset is created in early childhood as we learn, receive praise[1] and get assigned those inevitable labels as we develop and grow. Dweck's research uncovered two basic mindsets. A fixed mindset, where you believe you've inherited a particular set of abilities and are incapable of change, and a growth mindset, where you're open to change and think you can develop through focused effort and perseverance.

In my experience, Dweck was on the money, especially when it comes to business. Most clients I work with will have a very distinct money mindset and money story whether they realise it or not. And those beliefs, that story, feeds into every part of their business and how they manage their money.

Often, it's not until we uncover or address that money story or those limiting mindset beliefs that positive change starts to happen. That's why identifying your money story or set of beliefs and then dealing with those negative elements is essential to achieving success.

What's your business money mindset?

Where do you sit on the mindset scale? Do you have a fixed mindset or growth mindset, especially when it comes to business money?

Are you aware of those limiting beliefs?

And more importantly as you think about these things and write them down, are they true?

If you're not sure, consider this.

When you think about yourself, do you:

- Prefer to avoid challenges.

- Find it hard to accept failure or mistakes.

- Shy away from the unfamiliar areas in your business.

- Focus more on what you can do well or control.

- Struggle to learn new concepts, especially when it comes to money, so you don't even try?

If these describe you, you likely have a fixed mindset.

Not feeling the fixed mindset vibe? Then maybe you've got more of a growth mindset, especially if you:

- Accept the challenges in your business as opportunities to grow.

- Don't enjoy failing but tend to look for the learning opportunity in the failure.

- Dive into new areas of business with gusto.

- Find new concepts tricky but persevere and always ask for help.

However, if you see the challenges in your business as opportunities and you welcome the chance to learn and grow, especially following failure – or if you embrace learning new things, and dive into the unknown with enthusiasm, you've likely got a growth mindset.

Understanding where you sit on the mindset scale and identifying your money story is vital work because that information can help you over-come the limiting beliefs that might be holding you back. And while we're on the subject, no matter what your money mindset is right now, it's possible to change it at any time. That starts with letting go of what no longer serves you – rather than dwell on the past and make yourself feel bad about what you can't change, focus forward on what you can change and do that!

MONEY MAGNET TIP:

Grab a journal, sit in a quiet place, close your eyes and take a few deep breaths. As you sit in stillness, meditate on the mind-set questions above and try to determine what your money story is right now and where it came from. Then think about how this story impacts your mindset, the way you think and feel.

As you write, don't just take what's on paper at face value. Instead, dig deeper, ask yourself if that story you've been telling yourself is true. Can you find evidence that supports your story or is it simply that, a story that you've been telling yourself that no longer matters?

Why does mindset matter so much?

Now, this is definitely not a book on mindset. I'm no psychologist. Why then have I added an entire chapter on mindset in a business money book, and why does it even matter?

In my experience over many years in business, a negative, critical or limiting mindset is one of the most significant barriers to client success. In most cases, my clients weren't even aware that their unconscious mindset and self-biases were impacting their business.

However, as an outsider looking in, it was obvious. Fear of increasing prices just in case you lost potential clients; over-servicing and under-charging; giving away unprompted discounts; feeling like you have to 'pay your dues' before you earn a decent payday, the list goes on. Sound familiar?

That's why mindset matters, especially in business. Maintaining a positive, proactive, growth mindset can be the key to unlocking real success, particularly on the business finance front.

Your mindset directly impacts how you'll approach your business. You've heard the saying that you can't control what happens to you but can control how you react. So often in business, we find ourselves in reactive mode, playing catch up when we get the latest unexpected bill, wondering what to charge that new client or deciding what to do with the influx of cash. And while that might be due to a lack of planning, usually a fixed mindset or limiting self-belief is also to blame.

So, today is the day to switch things up! No matter what sort of mindset you have or how reactive your approach to business has been in the past, it's time to get proactive and embrace a growth mindset so you can be better prepared for the challenges that lie ahead. Let's enhance your critical thinking, kick those limiting beliefs to the curb so when those inevitable setbacks occur you'll stay motivated and focused on what's possible.

The journey starts TODAY!

What emotions or words do you associate with money, and how do they influence your financial decisions?

A) Fear and anxiety; I worry constantly about not having enough money.

B) Confidence and determination; I see money as a tool for achieving my goals.

C) Mixed feelings; sometimes I feel secure, other times uncertain.

What was your childhood experience with money?

A) We were always struggling to make ends meet.

B) I learned the value of hard work and resilience; to see opportunities instead of limitations.

C) I haven't thought much about how my past influences my present.

Does societal pressure play a part in your spending habits or impact your savings or financial goals?

A) I feel like I need to keep up with others, even if it means living beyond my means.

B) I focus on my own priorities and goals, regardless of what anyone else thinks.

C) On the fence about this, sometimes I feel the need to keep up with others and other times I stand my ground about money.

Do you prioritise saving versus spending?

A) I find it difficult to save; there's always something urgent to spend money on.

B) I make saving a priority and allocate a portion of my income to savings each month.

C) I'm unsure how to strike a balance between saving and spending; it varies depending on my circumstances.

How do you define financial success?

A) Financial success, ha, what's that?! I think I'll need to work forever!

B) Financial success means having the freedom to live life on my terms and I know I can get there!

C) I'm still figuring out what financial success means to me and how to work towards it.

There's been a major financial setback in your business or life. How do you respond?

A) Typical, I'm hopeless at this money stuff; I'll never get ahead financially.

B) Wow, that was a lot! How can I reassess my priorities and improve my financial habits so this never happens again?

C) I'm not sure what to do, maybe my accountant can help.

When you think about money, what are your main priorities?

A) Survival and security; I prioritise immediate needs over long-term goals.

B) I'm all about prioritising growth, abundance, and sustainability, these will guide my decisions towards achieving my long-term goals.

C) I consider various things when making financial decisions but haven't fully aligned them with my long-term goals yet.

How did you score?

MOSTLY As - Hey **Budget Boss! Y**ou have a keen eye for caution and a knack for saving every cent. While you're great at making ends meet, it's time to take those money smarts to the next level and sprinkle a little fun into your financial journey! Try adding some good money habits and work on a savings plan too!

MOSTLY Bs - OK, **Money Magnet!** You're unstoppable with your positive attitude and savvy money moves! Keep those big dreams alive and watch your wealth soar to new heights!

MOSTLY Cs - You're the **Financial Navigator** and when it comes to money you're steady and composed but remember, it's OK to ride the waves of opportunity every now and again!

What is stopping you from being wildly financially successful? (It could be your money story!)

'We each focus on what we're going to buy, but that's an incorrect focus. Focus instead on why you want to spend the money on this or that. What feeling in you does it satisfy?'

Suze Orman

Ah, money stories – have you heard of them before?

It's one of those things I'd never heard of until about 10 years ago when a friend pointed out my money story or behaviour around money.

So, what's a money story?

Money stories like mindset are usually formed when you're a child. Often based on cultural beliefs and passed down through generations; they are the beliefs, stories or feelings about money that are shared or experienced within families and communities.

Often, we unconsciously carry our money stories with us from childhood into adulthood, and they frame and impact our money decisions, from what we earn to how we spend.

My money story

My money story is a fairly common one; it's all about scarcity and definitely started for me as a child. My family never seemed to have money; my mum worked two jobs, and as kids, we began work at a very young age. Our family was constantly being chased for overdue bills, and we were under no illusion that money was a tight, finite commodity. We often heard the phrase *'money doesn't grow on trees'* when asking for something new and rarely had anything extra.

So, throughout my life, particularly when I started my first business, I carried my money story along for the ride; I just wasn't aware it was a passenger. It meant I did every task myself, and I mean everything. I would rather work a 60-hour week than outsource because I lived with the belief that money was scarce, even if it wasn't. I felt that I couldn't afford to pay a contractor (I could), and I'd probably do a better job myself anyway (jury is out on that one).

You can imagine how quickly and often that led to overwhelm and inevitably burn-out.

Honestly, though, when my friend pointed out my money story – that I was overly generous with everyone else but a tight-arse when it came to myself and my business – I thought it was a bit of nonsense. So, she sent me a quiz by Kendall Summerhawk, a US Business Coach, to justify her point of view.

I love quizzes, so I took Kendall's Money Personality quiz[2], and the outcome was an eye-opener. My money type is the Accumulator, a penny-pinching bargain hunter and conscious money saver who often gets stuck in analysis paralysis and perfectionism. Sounds awful, right? But in my heart, I knew it was true.

How did I react? Well, here's the thing, and it's what we all tend to do when we find out something about ourselves; we only believe part of the story, and it's usually the negative. That's absolutely what I did.

I didn't want to be a penny-pinching business grinch, so my immediate reaction was that I needed to start spending to change my story. Thankfully, though, cool heads prevailed, and I decided to do some self-reflection, trying to uncover why I was such an 'Accumulator' and why I was so afraid of being broke. I realised it was because I'd spent the first 17 years of my life conditioned to scarcity, and it was time to acknowledge the past so I could move forward.

I also realised that my story was not just negative; there were many positives to draw from and incorporate into a new money story as I went forward.

The biggest aha for me was that I'm a person who likes to have a handle on the debt, and that's okay. I feel comfortable and happy when I've got a nest egg in the bank and stressed out of my head when the amount going out is greater than the amount coming in. And while it makes me risk-averse, which often means I don't invest in myself and my business when I should, on the plus side, when it comes to money, I want to understand how it can help take my business to the next level, so I always keep an eye on the numbers.

The exciting thing in all of this is that since acknowledging my money story and embracing its pros and cons, I've managed to make more money and have a better business. In early 2023, I sold part of my business, something the 'Accumulator' in me would never even consider.

Can you identify a behaviour impacting your financial success, stifling your decision-making, or decreasing your growth potential or financial confidence? Can you link it back to a time in your life?

MONEY MAGNET TIP:

Becoming aware of your money story can help you take steps to challenge the limiting beliefs you're holding on to and help you develop a healthier, more positive relationship with money. This can increase financial confidence and decision-making and help you become wildly financially successful.

It's time to uncover your money story!

Put it into practice:

Now it's your turn; what's your money story?

Is your money story impacting your business?

Here are some money stories we often tell ourselves. Can you see yourself here?

- 'I don't have enough money, so I can't afford it.'

- 'I deserve to splurge and treat myself.'

- 'I'll never be able to retire comfortably.'

- 'I can't invest because I don't have much money.'

- 'I work hard for my money, so I should enjoy it.'

- 'I'll never be able to pay off my debt.'

- 'I don't do numbers!'

- 'I'm not good with money; I'll always struggle financially.'

- 'Money can't buy happiness.'

- 'I'll never be wealthy.'

- 'I have to live pay check to pay check.'

- 'I don't deserve it!'

Want to know your money type? See the examples below to determine how your money story might impact your business.

- **Spender vs. Saver:** People who prioritise spending and enjoying their money versus those prioritise saving and avoiding debt.

- **Risk-taker vs. Risk-averse:** People willing to take financial risks to achieve higher returns versus those who prefer to play it safe with their investments.

- **Impulsive vs. Deliberate:** People who make impulsive financial decisions versus those who take a more thoughtful and calculated approach.

- **Money-focused vs. Value-focused:** People who prioritise financial success and material possessions versus those who prioritise personal values and experiences.

- **Hoarder vs. Giver:** People who hoard their money and resources versus those who are generous with their money and give to others.

Once you uncover your money story and type, you'll better understand how your mindset and money story might impact your business.

When you see negative behaviour, for example, you're spending way more than you earn or you're not saving for a rainy day, write it down, become conscious of the way you interact with money and then, before you make any decisions, ask yourself:

- Why am I reacting this way? Do I really need to make that purchase? Is this something I need, or is it a response to stress, for example.

- Will this benefit me now and in the long term?

- Am I being proactive or reactive in this situation?

- Is what I'm telling myself true?

Imposter syndrome and how to overcome limiting beliefs

Let's talk about imposter syndrome for a minute because it just might be the growing epidemic among women in business this decade.

Imposter syndrome shows up for all of us at some point in our business journey. If you're unsure what I mean by imposter syndrome, essentially, it's that nagging feeling that you don't really deserve a seat at the table, the win you just had, ah, it must be a fluke, and it's only a matter of time before someone discovers you're not actually everything you claim to be, because you're just ... *<insert the limiting belief here>*.

It seems that hand in hand with imposter syndrome comes a healthy dose of comparisonitis; the constant need to compare yourself and your business to another business or business owner. You know, the one over there kicking goals or the seemingly successful entrepreneur on social media who seems to kick goals every single week, leaving you wondering why you can't do that too?

After years of working with so many fabulous business owners, it's evident that imposter syndrome often comes with the territory, especially if you're a woman in business. On some level, you don't think you deserve success or to be in the game – full stop. You're hell-bent on sabotaging yourself at every turn and comparing yourself to everyone else makes it just that bit easier.

While there's no single or simple cause of imposter syndrome, things like upbringing, culture, and your current environment are likely factors in determining why you feel the way you feel. Left unchecked, imposter syndrome and buying into those limiting beliefs or stories we tell ourselves can significantly impact our lives and businesses. Not only does it hurt our mental health, but in the most extreme cases, it can stop us from showing up, speaking up and reaching our success goals.

So next time you start to doubt yourself, think you don't deserve to charge that much or take your well-earned seat at the table, here are some tips to overcome those negative thoughts, say goodbye to imposter syndrome, and limiting beliefs for good.

1. Remind yourself that you're in the right place. It's the right time, and your business is exactly where it needs to be right now. As you learn, grow, and gain confidence, you'll change, and so will your business, and that's okay.

2. Celebrate your successes! No matter how big or how small, when you achieve something, take the time and celebrate your success. Your celebration doesn't have to be extravagant or cost a lot of money; it's about acknowledging what you've achieved and knowing there's more where that came from.

3. Start a success journal and note every win in your business. When

imposter syndrome creeps in, or you're tempted to let those limiting beliefs stop you in your tracks, reading back over your wins, especially when things aren't going your way, will give you a much-needed boost.

4. Understand that business ebbs and flows; it's not all going to be big wins and sunshine all the time. The lows don't make you a bad business owner or undermine your skills. Instead, reframe when there's a hiccup or, worse, if you fail; view it as an opportunity to learn and grow.

5. Surround yourself with a fantastic community or gang of cheer-leaders. No negative energy is allowed! And just as your business gang supports you, return the favour and support them, too.

6. Ask for help! Look for a business mentor or coach who can help you get from where you are now to where you want to be. Choose someone who understands business because they've been there, done that and who can genuinely help you reach your goals. You might need empathy, but strategy is just as important.

7. Take care of yourself! Often, imposter syndrome is at its worst in situations of high stress. So, try to find ways to manage your stress and take time out of your business when needed. You could choose something simple like a daily meditation, walk in the park or spend time writing in a journal. The magic is in understanding what you can change in those imposter syndrome moments so you can stop comparing yourself to everyone else and be uniquely you.

And if you're thinking that overcoming imposter syndrome and limiting beliefs is easier said than done, consider my client Grace for a moment. When I first met Grace, she was almost paralysed with fear about her business – from the finances to the product she delivered, she believed that every step on her business journey could be the step that ended it all.

As we talked through the anxiety that surrounded Grace and how she felt about her business, it became clear that she felt like an industry imposter. Although Grace had almost 25 years in the bank as an educator, as a new business owner she felt completely out of her depth. Grace spent a lot of time comparing herself to others in her industry. Many of these educators had far less experience than Grace, but because they were well ahead on their business journey, Grace felt like she didn't deserve a seat at the table.

So, what did we do next?

It was pretty simple really.

We made a list of what Grace had to offer – all of the value she could bring to her clients and why her wealth of experience was vital in her industry and needed to be shared.

Then we did a SWOT analysis of her business and made a list of where the business side of things needed to improve – adding systems and processes and outsourcing tasks were big ones.

Then, we examined each of the thoughts Grace had about herself and her business when that imposter syndrome took hold. As she wrote them down, I asked her to consider if they were true or not, to do the research and find the evidence one way or another.

Finally, Grace built in a morning routine that set her up for the day – she included meditation and journaling and addressed the negative self-talk that she often entertained. In addition, Grace added a success and gratitude journaling session to her week. While it wasn't a practice she wanted to do every day, Grace carried the journal with her so she could write in it when the need arose.

The result. Within a few months Grace felt better about herself and her business. She embraced the value her experience brought to the table and understood that while her business was a work in progress, it didn't mean that she was an industry imposter.

Now, five years later, Grace has become a go-to mentor in her industry for new educators who feel a little lost or like they don't belong. I'd call that a win!

Why you need confidence to help your business grow

Business is about confidence. And building business confidence is like building muscle – it takes consistency and time. It also takes a proactive growth mindset, particularly regarding finances, so continually working on your mindset will also help you increase your confidence.

About four years ago, I started working with a new client. Bianca was a talented designer, had been in the business for almost 15 years and got most of her work through referrals from happy clients. But, despite 40-plus-hour weeks spent on the job, Bianca made enough money to cover her business costs but very little left over to show for her hard work. In fact, she was barely taking $20,000 in wages each year; that's less than $10 an hour (before tax)!

Bianca also felt tied to her business and not in a good way. While she usually worked 40 hours a week in her company, she felt like she was on the business treadmill 24/7, 365. There were no holidays and very little family time, and her accountant kept telling her to give up her 'hobby' because her hubby had a great job. Wouldn't she prefer to go out and have lunch with the girls?!

I'll always remember that first emotional phone call with Bianca. She believed in her skills and what she could offer her clients. She loved her job, the design process and creating something beautiful for her customers, but she needed more confidence.

Whenever she spoke to her accountant, she felt like a fool, and when Bianca talked about business with her friends, her insecurities shone through. Maybe she shouldn't be working in a space where there were so many other successful, prominent designers competing for the same jobs. Her family felt neglected, and Bianca felt terrible all the time. Plus, there was the constant worry over whether she would make enough to pay her business costs and tax obligations. Despite her love for her work, her business held very little joy.

Then the unthinkable happened. Bianca's hubby was made redundant, and his hefty salary disappeared overnight. They'd blown through the redundancy payout and Covid had just kicked off, and no one was hiring. Suddenly, Bianca's business needed to step up, and she came to me looking for a miracle.

Now, I'm no miracle worker, that's for sure, but it became apparent pretty quickly where the issue was in Bianca's business. A design veteran, Bianca charged her clients an hourly rate of about one-quarter that of her competitors. Why? That's what she charged when she started her business, and she never considered a price increase – despite her skill and experience increasing over her many years in business.

My immediate reaction was relief for Bianca and for me because, hey, as I said, I'm no miracle worker. This would be a simple fix; we'd review Bianca's service model, increase her prices and see an immediate improvement in her business.

What I underestimated at the time was Bianca's complete lack of confidence. It was heart-wrenching when she told me that her prices had never increased because she didn't believe she deserved to earn more and was afraid of losing clients. But to her credit, Bianca was determined;

she was now the sole earner in her family, the breadwinner, and she had to make her business work.

We didn't muck about. We ripped off the bandaid, immediately increased Bianca's prices across the board to market rates, improved her quoting process, and implemented progress payments for each project, so there was always cash flow.

And, we worked on her confidence. Bianca's business boomed. Because she was now more expensive, she became a magnet for new business; the perception that expensive equals better quality and service.

Before long, Bianca hired help, and by the end of that financial year, she was not only turning over a quarter of a million dollars, but her salary had increased to $90,000 per annum.

Twelve months later, we rounded off our second financial year working together with half a million dollars in turnover, a salary of $160,000 and a business profit of more than 20 percent.

Bianca had a renewed confidence in herself and her worth as a designer. Now, years later, she turns away work because she chooses to work half as much while earning the same money.

All of this didn't just happen. Bianca worked hard building her confidence muscle. Between daily meditations, constant reminders from me and the support of a group of savvy designer friends, Bianca was constantly reminded what she could achieve by silencing the imposter syndrome, choosing who she wanted to work with and backing herself and her ability in business.

Flexing your mindset muscle

'You get what you focus on, so focus on what you want.'

Jeremy McGilvrey

As you're probably picking up on by now, mindset matters, particularly in business – and because a healthy and positive mindset is crucial to business success, I called in a couple of my qualified business friends, the big guns when it comes to mindset, to give their tips.

A huge thanks to Shannah Kennedy, Master Life Coach and Life Planner and Kerry Rowett, Kinesiologist and Intuitive Business Mentor, for sharing their thoughts.

Shannah Kennedy:

Why does mindset matter, particularly regarding the financial side of business?

'Mindset is a pivotal factor in the financial side of business due to its influence on decision-making, risk-taking, and resilience. A growth-oriented mindset fosters adaptability and a willingness to innovate, which is crucial in navigating dynamic markets and seizing new opportunities. Conversely, a fixed or limited mindset may hinder strategic thinking, leading to an aversion to risks and missed chances for growth.'

'A positive financial mindset encourages learning from failures, embracing calculated risks, and maintaining a long-term perspective, key elements for enduring success in the volatile landscape of business finances.'

So many of us have a money story that leads to limiting beliefs and money mindset blocks. How can we uncover our money story?

'Exploring our money story often begins by reflecting on childhood experiences, family attitudes toward money, and past financial challenges. It involves examining our beliefs about wealth, success, and self-worth.'

'Journaling, seeking therapy or coaching, and discussing money openly with trusted individuals can unearth patterns and beliefs shaping our financial mindset. Questioning our reactions to financial situations and identifying recurring thoughts about money helps us understand our money story and reveal limiting beliefs or blocks that influence our relationship with finances.'

Why does our money story stop us from becoming financially successful, and how can we overcome a 'bad' money story?

'Our money story often contains deeply ingrained beliefs about wealth, success, and our own capabilities, which can create self-imposed limitations on financial success. Overcoming a 'bad' money story involves recognising these limiting beliefs and actively reframing them. One approach is challenging negative beliefs by seeking evidence that contradicts them. Set specific financial goals, create a realistic plan to achieve them, and celebrate small victories to reinforce positive beliefs about your financial abilities.'

'Regularly reassess and adjust your money story, replacing limiting beliefs with empowering ones to prevent them from sabotaging your financial success.'

How can we build our confidence muscle when it comes to business finance?

'Building confidence in business finance involves several steps. Start by educating yourself about financial concepts relevant to your business. This could mean taking courses, reading books, or seeking mentorship.

Practice applying these concepts in real-life scenarios by managing a budget or analysing financial statements. Embrace learning from successes and mistakes, as this hands-on experience strengthens your financial acumen.

Surround yourself with a supportive network of finance professionals or mentors who can offer guidance and feedback. Gradually, as you gain more knowledge and experience, your confidence in handling business finances will grow.'

Kerry Rowett:

Why does mindset matter, particularly regarding the financial side of business?

'The problem with a poor mindset is its impact on your behaviour – and in business, poor behaviours and habits can lead to a lot of financial stress. If you fear money and avoid looking at your bank accounts or profitability – it's hard to make good money decisions.'

'If you believe you'll never be good with money, you'll avoid learning and taking action to help you improve. If your mindset is based on denial, you ignore what feels boring, won't plan ahead and can experience some rude shocks.'

'The good news is that you can create a good mindset. As you learn and become better with money, you have the power to create change and improve your mindset.'

So many of us have a money story that leads to limiting beliefs and money mindset blocks. How can we uncover our money story?

'You can start to uncover your money story by noticing what you say and think about money. You might make an offhand comment like, "Making money is hard work," or perhaps you find yourself saying, "Money is harder for people like me because ..." You might feel entirely invested in your belief like it really *is* true. You might have a lot of evidence to back it up.'

'But, instead of further reinforcing the belief, you might pause and ask yourself: "Whose belief is this?" or "Where does this come from?"'

'If you can identify someone or a circumstance from your childhood – bingo. You have likely hit upon a money story. The first step is recognising that it is indeed a story and that this story still impacts you today. Inequality, injustice, trauma, poverty, discrimination – these things are all very real. If any are part of your money story, you may have more layers of healing to do.'

'Whatever your circumstance or story, you might ask yourself, "Am I ready and willing to create a new, empowering, triumphant money story from here?"'

Why does our money story stop us from becoming financially successful, and how can we overcome a 'bad' money story?

'Our money story blocks us when we view it as an immutable part of our identity. It just "is" and can't be changed. We might feel powerless to change it. Old patterns persist, and we can find ourselves back in a bad place with money despite our best efforts.'

'A common pattern I see is the feast and famine cycles in business. The bad money story might be, "Money is a rollercoaster for me; it always has been." It's helpful to understand the origins of the pattern to break this kind of pattern. Did this pattern show up in your childhood? When did it begin? From there, it's also important to consider what needs to change to break the cycle. For example, excessive focus on "thinking abundantly" when things are going well can lead to overspending rather than considering investments and setting money aside for future slower periods, holidays, unforeseen expenses, and increased tax commitments.'

How can we build our confidence muscle when it comes to business finance?

'Developing your competence will build your confidence – this is called the confidence/competence loop. Learn more about money (which you're doing right now!), get the proper support (a helpful accountant and bookkeeper, additional support for your mindset if you need it), put into place processes (like direct debits and transfers, for example to a tax account) and over time, your confidence around money will grow.

'Returning to our growth mindset, there will always be more to learn. As your business grows, tax planning or cash flow management might become more complex, and different investment opportunities open up – embrace ongoing learning.'

Chapter 4

How to Create a Winning Financial Plan

'It takes as much energy to wish as it does to plan.'

Eleanor Roosevelt

If you've been in business for a while, you've probably either taken a planning workshop, heard other business owners speak about the value in their planning sessions, or you've put 'must do some planning' on your to-do list. It's one of those things we refer to when we speak about working *on* the business rather than *in* the business.

I'm definitely one of those business owners who loves a planning session. Over the years, I've become disciplined about getting my plan or focus down on paper because, in my case, if I don't have something concrete written down, I'll create a bunch of endless to-do lists and waste an excessive amount of time in procrastination mode. So, at the end of each quarter, sometimes even each month, I create a forward plan. It all depends on how frantic business has been.

However, when it comes to creating a plan for my business, where I differ from other business owners is I *always* include a financial goal.

I have an overarching financial goal for the quarter, usually tied to how much I want to earn. Then, I build a smaller financial goal for each month. Having a plan that includes a financial focus has been a game-changer for me.

Do you really need a plan?

The simple answer to that is no.

But, in my experience, creating a plan is the way to create the most success and profit in your business.

When I was navigating our overwhelming tax debt, creating a plan and having a list of bite-sized financial goals was the difference between constant overwhelm and wanting to give up, and moving forward.

Over the years, I've seen business planning in action many times and I know it works. But even if planning is something you've never entertained, I'd recommend you give it a go just once and see if it makes a difference.

In my experience, creating a plan will help you:

- Gain clarity – as you define and refine your business and your definition of success.

- Create a clear and determined path forward – instead of being swept along for the ride in the day-to-day; it's all about getting proactive!

- Reframe your thinking – so you can avoid being overwhelmed and become 'unstuck'.

- Be inspired or re-inspired in your business.

If nothing changes, nothing changes.

You've already done some of the work in the success chapter of the book, so now, spend an hour creating a plan for the next quarter and see for yourself what a difference it makes.

How to create your winning financial plan

When planning, most of us give up before we even start. It's usually because we don't have the time. Either there are a hundred more pressing priorities, or to do a plan justice you need to book yourself into a hotel, take a mini vacation and get out of the office, right?

And while you definitely need to make the time, you absolutely do not need the mini-vacay, no matter how appealing it seems.

We all know we've all got the same hours in the day as Beyoncé, but in reality, we probably lack the budget and hired-help to spend our time doing whatever we want. I definitely fit into that camp. So, when I started my business planning sessions as a solopreneur with four small boys to care for, I wanted to make the process as simple as possible. I'd find an hour once a month, put it in the diary and make the time non-negotiable.

Put it into practice:

In this exercise, start with at least one main financial goal. *Let's review:*

What worked? Thinking back over the last quarter, write down three wins, especially the ones you enjoyed or want to experience again.

1.

2.

3.

For example: Was there a service you loved delivering, a quick-win that made you money, a client win or a great testimonial?

What didn't go to plan? Write down three things that didn't go to plan, you didn't enjoy and would rather not repeat.

1.

2.

3.

For example: Is there a product or service that's costing too much to deliver, an area of business that's sucking your time and could be out-sourced, or an unexpected bill that dents the cash flow?

What lessons did you learn? Make a note of the lessons you learned, things you need to do differently next time or how you felt.

1.

2.

3.

For example:

- Have you discovered a problem with your systems and processes that's putting a handbrake on your growth?

- Is there a product or service you need to stop or change to suit the current market?

- Did you discover the kind of client you love working with so now know it's time to review your ideal client avatar?

- Do you need to modify how you work because you're over-whelmed, or are you unhappy in your business?

> **MONEY MAGNET TIP:**
>
> Make this one-hour review in your business NON-NEGOTIABLE each month. It might take some juggling, but I know you can absolutely find an hour. Even if you're planning for an entire quarter, planning in smaller chunks and spending an hour each month will make the task less daunting and more manageable.
>
> Checking in monthly also allows you to be more agile too. Go find that hour!

What would you do if you knew you couldn't fail?

It's a big, sweeping question I like to ask myself every month.

And now, I ask that question of you: as you go into the next quarter, what would you do or try to achieve if you knew anything was possible?

Your answer to this question becomes the basis of your goal.

This is often where the roadblock occurs in the process, so if you feel overwhelmed by the question, ask yourself this instead: *What's the one thing you could do right now to move the needle forward in your business?*

Aim big, but think small. Talk it over with a business friend, or say it out loud!

To achieve this goal, what outside factors do you need to consider as you make your plans? What season of life/business are you in right now? For example, the kids are on holiday; you've got a full schedule of 1:1 clients; it's traditionally a busy/quiet time in business.

Then consider: what can and will you achieve in the next 30, 60 or 90 days?

Most business owners come unstuck here because they want to achieve a laundry list of goals rather than a single focus. So decide. Do you want to achieve – one big thing or lots of little things? If your big goal will take you more than a few months or seems too overwhelming, then break it down into smaller bite-sized goals and start with those. But no matter what you do, don't get carried away, and never pick more than three goals for a period.

Stuck on choosing a strong financial goal?

A financial goal is a must-have when creating business goals.

Whether it's finally reaching those seven-figures, ending the quarter with a higher net profit, paying yourself, adding a few hundred or thousands (or tens of thousands) of dollars to savings, or simply getting better organised and being more accountable when it comes to the business finances, a financial goal will keep you focused and on track to achieve business success.

No matter what business season you're in, if you're not making money, you potentially have a time-consuming hobby rather than a business.

Let's be honest; none of us want to work for free, no matter how passionate we feel about our business. So, when answering this question, have your financial goal front and centre.

Stuck for a financial goal? Consider these prompts to help you get clear:

- Get a handle on your business numbers – how much do you earn and how much do you spend?

- Have a better understanding of the business metrics, like profit margins, conversion rates, customer retention.

- Understand your compliance obligations – the what and when and how much!

- Create or start rainy-day savings.

- Conduct a pricing review and work out the best way to communicate it to your clients.

- Find a financial partner, accountant, bookkeeper or mentor who can help the business grow.

- Create some 'quick-win' products to boost cash flow.

- Start paying yourself a regular wage and superannuation, too.

When choosing your goals, remember:

- Your goals can be short-term or long-term.

- Goals need to be clear, focused, practical and realistic.

- Your goals should always be measurable so you know if you're getting the results you want to achieve, and finally ...

- Your goals list must include a financial or 'numbers' goal because everything else will fall into place when the focus is on the numbers.

Let's create your plan

Now you've decided on your goals, it's time to create a plan. These are the specific action steps you need to achieve your goals.

For example – your goal might be to get a handle on your numbers in the next quarter. So, to achieve this, your plan might look like this:

Month one:

1. Check that your business account is a business-only bank account, and you're not spending on personal expenses.

2. Open a linked business savings account and a business tax savings account.

3. Introduce cloud accounting into the business and link those accounts to your cloud accounting system.

Month two:

1. Look at the business cash flow. Where is the money coming from and going to?

2. Work out what it costs to run the business.

3. Create a cash flow document and understand where you need to save for upcoming bills and where you can spend.

Month three:

1. Look at each business service, how long it takes to deliver the service and whether the service is making a profit.

2. Decide on your profit number. Your profit is the money left over after you've covered all your business costs. We'll chat about profit throughout the book but check out chapter 12.

3. Review your prices. Compare against competitors and review your history to see when you last increased your prices.

Once you know what you need to do, what steps will you take to achieve each outcome?

Think about the basics here. Write these down and consider what you need to do yourself, what you can delegate and what's nice to do on the list but not really necessary (when you come up with these, hit the dump button).

Now you've got the specifics, the next step is to plan when you will do each action.

- Schedule a time and write each step in the diary or on a white-board or use project management software like monday.com or Asana.

- Delegate to staff or contractions where needed and provide clear instructions and expectations.

- Set task deadlines; and finally …

- Follow up! Have regular 'Work In Progress' meetings and create clear communication channels so the project keeps moving forward.

How will you know if you've achieved your goals?

Doing this work, creating goals and putting action plans in place is one thing. But often, the process gets hijacked or forgotten when business gets busy or because you don't know how to measure your goals or don't put clear deadlines in place.

When you create a goal, understand from the get-go how you'll measure it and when you want to complete it (i.e. set a deadline) because it's the only way you'll stay on track and know if you've achieved your goal.

For example:

Goal: To improve the key financial metrics in my business.

Action step: Take a baseline of the numbers you intend to measure. In this case, you'll measure:

- The dollars in the bank.

- The net profit number on the profit and loss statement.

- The average number of new customers per month.

- The number of returning customers each month.

- The number of new subscribers on the mailing list.

- The social media numbers.

Deadline: 30 days

Success means: Improving each of these numbers/areas by at least 1 percent.

MONEY MAGNET TIPS FOR SUCCESS!

1. Put your goals front and centre so you can see them every day.

2. Have clear deadlines and write them down. Put a reminder in your phone or on your calendar.

3. Conduct regular reviews.

4. If you don't have a team, get an accountability buddy – a coach or a business friend to help you stay on track.

5. And remember, a little progress each day adds up to BIG results!

Business Money
Foundations

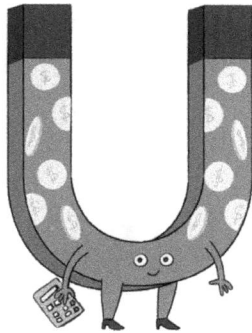

Chapter 5

Building Strong Financial Foundations

'A big part of financial freedom is having your heart and mind free from worry about the what-ifs of life.'

Suze Orman

Once upon a time, being financially free meant owning a house.

Even if that house came with a hefty mortgage, the idea of home ownership meant you'd achieved a financial milestone, and in some ways, it meant you'd made it. It was a sign you'd come of age financially speaking, and you had the world at your feet.

However, in recent years, as home ownership becomes more a mission impossible than a dream, achieving financial freedom is still on the top of the business and lifestyle priority list – but the definition is different. Now, it's all about financial security and accumulating enough resources to build on opportunities and optimise your business and life. And in the dream scenario, enough resources to cover living expenses without needing to rely on employment!

We're chasing financial freedom harder than ever.

And we're diversifying income streams, investing, creating side hustles upon side hustles and starting small businesses at lightning speed.

According to the Australian Bureau of Statistics (ABS), over 2.5 million small businesses are actively trading in Australia[3] and in the USA, the US Small Business Administration (SBA) reports that over 33.2 million small businesses are in operation[4]. In Australia, nearly 50 percent of these small businesses started post-2020.

When you look at the stats, there's no doubt that small businesses have become the backbone of most western economies.

But the reality is that one in five small businesses and side hustles will fail within the first year of business. About 38 percent of those businesses fail because they need more money. A survey from QuickBooks[5] suggests that more than 40 percent of small business owners identify as financially illiterate or having little or no clue about the money side of the business.

The really bad news? It's an epidemic on the rise.

Lack of financial literacy has become one of the biggest roadblocks to small business success.

As small business numbers increase, there continues to be a sharp decline in financial literacy[6]. Why? Let's be honest – no one decides to open a business to do the numbers. We open businesses because we're excited to work for ourselves, do something we love, and to offer the service or create the product that we know will make a difference and transform our customers' lives, that will feed our soul and create the lifestyle we've always dreamed of having. And while we know there's money involved somewhere, at face value, it seems complicated. Ignoring the business money is often easier than facing reality.

So, when conceiving business ideas, very few people will sit down and do a budget, cash flow and financial forecast for business success. The numbers just aren't that sexy! We'd much rather be doing the fun stuff. Choosing fonts and colours for websites, doing logo designs or working out clever ways to market our product all sit at the top of the list and well above the finances. Honestly, at the start of the business journey, everything is more fun than the numbers ... until it isn't!

Like it or not, the keys to business viability, sustainability and growth are things like sound financial management, understanding cash flow, pricing and profits, having sound financial systems and processes in place and building strong financial foundations.

Even if you don't do numbers or you plan to outsource your finances, as a business owner, you must take the time to understand the business money and improve your financial literacy. Because when you do, magic happens!

Boosting business confidence

For starters, understanding the finance basics will help you increase your money muscle and confidence. You'll not only be able to manage your finances more effectively, but when you understand the basics, you're more likely to keep a regular eye on the money, set financial goals and make better, informed decisions about buying, selling and investing in your business. Better decisions lead to better outcomes, and better outcomes lead to success. And we're all here for success!

As you increase your business money knowledge, that dreaded quarterly or year-end meeting with your accountant will become a breeze. When you're thinking about the next collaboration, chatting with your suppliers or wondering if now is the time to add a new income stream or staff member, you'll make decisions based on financial fact rather than guesswork.

You'll understand when you can hire, when you can invest in equipment or new tech, and when you need to pull back.

But best of all, when you know what's going on with the business money, you'll always have your eye on the prize, and even if you don't manage the finances day-to-day, you'll understand what it takes to achieve your goals and have a clear vision of how you'll get there and by when. Plus, you'll never wonder where all the money has gone again.

The bottom line is that increasing financial literacy will help you on your journey to financial freedom. And, while you may never have as much money as Oprah or Taylor, you might have enough to create the life (and business) of your dreams. That's a goal worth striving towards!

So, in this section of the book, we're diving into the basics of business money, all the things you need to build solid financial foundations so your business can thrive, not just survive.

If you stop at this section, you'll understand all the foundations you need to create a financially strong business, one that will weather the storm and set you up for future success.

MONEY MAGNET TIP

No matter who you are, where you are on your business money journey or what your relationship is with money, it's possible to understand your finances – the trick is to not get overwhelmed in the process.

So, as you embark on your journey to increase your financial literacy and improve the financial side of your business, take your time. Give yourself permission to make mistakes, ask all the questions, even if you think they're silly (there's no such thing by the way!) and eventually, you will get better at understanding where you are now and where you want to go. It's all about persistence and being kind to yourself!

Chapter 6

Business Bank Accounts 101

One of the most common questions I get asked is about business bank accounts: how many accounts do you really need, why do you need them, and how do you manage them?

While there are many answers to the question, from a single account to the five-plus accounts suggested by Profit First aficionados, the truth is that no matter how many accounts you have, business bank accounts make life easier when used *only* for business purposes. That goes double for a credit card!

Now, in most countries, if you're operating your business as an individual or sole trader, you're not required to have a business bank account per se. However, if you're operating as a Pty Ltd company (LLC/PLC), partnership, or trust, you're legally required to have a dedicated business-only bank account for tax purposes.

The way I look at it, no matter what entity you're running, you need to open a dedicated business-only account if you're in business.

Here's why:

- Your business bank account is good for your business mindset. It's another signal to yourself that you're a business owner and take the business money seriously.

- A business-only bank account helps you track all your income and expenses and allows you to check your day-to-day cash flow at a glance.

- Your finance professionals will thank you. When tax time rolls around, you can account for all your business transactions in one place.

- Record keeping will be a breeze, as you'll save time and money on record keeping and help your accountant or bookkeeper give you better advice.

- Your business bank account is an asset, so if you ever want to scale your business and need a loan or decide to sell your business, presenting details from a single dedicated business-only account looks professional and helps make your finances easier to understand.

When it comes to business bank accounts, I am like Goldilocks: I think three business accounts are just right.

Three separate business bank accounts make life easy. They help streamline business money and simplify business savings. The three essential business accounts are:

- an operating account

- a savings account for tax and superannuation expenses (your compliance)

- an additional savings account for emergencies, let's call it your rainy day account.

Opening multiple business accounts is usually straightforward because, unless you're a company, trust or partnership, you can do it all online.

Once you've opened your operating account, most financial institutions allow you to open additional, linked 'online only' accounts, in just a few clicks. I look for fee-free linked accounts that pay a good interest rate because they make outstanding business savings accounts. As the name suggests, these 'online only' accounts are only accessible via Internet banking. You can't withdraw funds at an ATM, so it takes out the temptation to use the saved funds for a spur-of-the-moment purchase, and that's a real plus.

The Operating Account

The operating account is your primary business account. All of your income and all of your expenses will go through this account. The operating account is where:

- Your clients will pay you, and you'll receive all your business income.

- You'll connect your payment facilities like Stripe and PayPal.

- You'll pay all of your business bills.

- You'll make monthly payments to your business-only credit card if you have one.

- Your business debit card, if you have one, is linked.

- You'll pay the business wages for yourself, staff and contractors.

- You'll transfer money to linked accounts to cover savings for tax, superannuation and other compliance.

- If you have one, you'll transfer money to a linked rainy day, emergency or profit account.

Your operating account is an essential cog in the engine room of your business finances, so it's also vital to ensure that you link this account, as the primary account, to your cloud accounting software and that the bank feeds are working. I'd suggest linking all of your business accounts to your cloud accounting software because it makes life, and accounting for money, easier.

MONEY MAGNET TIP:

To differentiate your business direct debit card from your other debit cards, use a sticker or add a dollop of brightly coloured nail varnish to the corner of the business debit card. That way, you'll be less likely to grab the wrong card at the store.

The Tax Account

It's tax time, and you get the news you've been dreading – you owe money in taxes or other business compliance, but you don't have enough to pay the bill!

I know first-hand how stressful it is to be in that position, and, at the moment it happened to me, I decided never to be caught out again. That's why one of the first things I added to my arsenal was a save-as-you-go approach to business taxes. Saving for tax has brought me peace of mind over the years, and I guarantee it will do the same for you.

So, your second must-have business bank account is a tax savings account. If you already have a tax bank account, here's a high-five. But if you don't have a business tax account, stop reading and open one. Right now! Open a high-interest, no-fee account linked to your business account and start saving.

Now, you're probably wondering how much you need to save and how often you should deposit that money into your tax account, and my advice is to keep it simple.

Here are some ways to save for your business taxes; pick one or two, but whatever you decide, make sure you're consistent.

First, understand your tax obligations, what you'll pay, and when. There are many different business taxes and compliance obligations, so speak to your financial partner and get a handle on potential liabilities and what you'll need to save. When you know, you can choose the best way to focus on savings.

For example: In Australia, businesses must register for Goods and Services Tax (GST) once business turnover reaches $75K in a financial year. So, all GST-registered businesses must add a 10 percent tax on top of their product or service costs when invoicing.

At the end of each quarter during the financial year, a GST-registered business must remit any GST they've collected, less any GST credits, to the Government. In this example, to keep saving for GST simple, calculate 10% of the total income received into your operating account each week and transfer that amount into your tax savings account.

In most cases, saving for GST this way means you'll save more money than you need to pay your GST compliance. But, once you pay your tax obligations, those extra funds can build a buffer for the next compliance bill, be taken as a bonus, pay increase or reinvested in the business.

If you have staff and collect tax from their wages or you need to pay them superannuation, calculate those amounts at the end of each pay cycle and immediately transfer the total into the tax savings account.

If you don't employ staff but know you need to pay tax for yourself at the end of the tax year, look back on your previous personal or company tax bill and estimate what you might need to pay. Divide the total by 52 and determine the weekly amount you'll need to transfer to cover your future tax.

Set up a direct weekly direct debit to your tax account using that amount. If things have changed in your business and you want a more accurate idea of what you might owe in taxes, use one of the handy tax calculators available online or speak to your tax professional.

So often, when the cash flow dwindles, the first thing to go is saving, but saving for compliance means sanity in my books, and having one less business stress sounds fantastic, right?

The Rainy Day Account

Most business owners find this third account the toughest because when all is said and done, there never seems to be enough funds for savings. But, whether it's a business or a personal rainy day account, or one of each, I guarantee this account will come in handy when you least expect it. We all remember the pandemic!

Call it what you want; the rainy day account is essentially an emergency fund for when the going gets tough. Ideally, you'll want to save at least three months' worth of business expenses (that's everything it costs you to run your business, including your wages) in this account.

Once again, open a linked, fee-free, preferably high-interest earning account and give it a name that keeps you motivated to stay the course and keep saving. From the OMG Fund to the Holy F#*K Account to the $1K Account or the I'm Worth It Fund, I've seen some fantastic names used over the years. Not only does it gamify saving and make it fun, but using a dedicated bank account for emergency savings will change how you approach your business savings goals.

While having multiple bank accounts can seem like a chore, in my experience, using a multi-account system can help reduce accidental spending, ensure your government obligations are paid in full and on time, and make you think twice about taking money out of the business that isn't there. And if you use cloud accounting software, linking all of your business accounts will save you time and money and make life easier at tax time, too. Plus, it's also good for stress levels!

MONEY MAGNET TIP

I guarantee that the task will appear daunting at first, but like everything hard, break it down into small manageable chunks: $5 this week, $10 next week. You'll be surprised how quickly it adds it and how addictive the rainy day account becomes.

I started my rainy day account when we were in the midst of our tax debt, so I started by opening an account with a dollar and saving coins. Each week I'd head to the bank and make a deposit in coins; the Teller wasn't impressed. Eventually, coins became five-dollar notes and then, when the finances improved, a dedicated weekly direct debit.

Start small and grow big

But wait … there's one more!

Once you've got your three core accounts working well, or, if you're super organised and know this will be easy-breezy, I suggest you open a profit account. The business profit account is, as it sounds, for business profits.

Now, a lot of business owners won't open this account because working out profit can be difficult, but business profit can be fluid as money comes and goes. If you price your services and add a 20 percent profit target for example, or you use Profit First, then all you need to do is transfer your profit number as soon as the revenue hits your operating account.

It means taking more time to review the numbers, what's been paid and the dollars in the bank, but everyone I know who embraced the profit account has been thrilled with the outcome.

At the end of the financial year, those unencumbered funds can be used to pay yourself a bonus, reinvest in the business or add to savings.

Chapter 7

The Game-Changers and the Power of Good Systems and Processes

'If you can't describe what you are doing as a process, you don't know what you're doing.'

W. Edwards Deming

There's all sorts of magic in sound systems and processes, *especially* when they relate to money.

Whether they're the ones you incorporate into your life or your business, having effective and simple financial systems and procedures in place can be game changers, because they free up precious time and have the power to unlock your business's potential.

But, in my experience, when you're starting a business, incorporating systems and processes often gets added to the 'one-day' list – especially the financial ones.

Business owners are likely doing what needs to be done themselves because it's easier or faster, and writing down a process or bringing in a tech system to help streamline operations is often considered a waste of time or money. And that's okay – until it isn't!

At some stage, the business will grow, and that mundane or repetitive task will start eating into time that could be better spent doing what needs to be done to generate revenue or deliver services. That's when the wheels will begin to fall off.

Like it or not, you can't do it all and keeping that day-to-day knowledge in your head will inevitably slow things down, especially when you want to bring new team members on board.

So, no matter what stage of business you're at now, it is time to think about your current systems and processes. Where can they improve and help you optimise your precious time, increase productivity and help your business grow?

If you're not sure where to start or don't know when to add or improve your business systems and processes, here are some things to consider:

Are repetitive tasks taking over?

If you find yourself constantly stuck doing mundane, repetitive tasks that devour your time and energy, it's a clear sign that you need systems and processes, or your current ones need improving. Look for opportunities to automate or delegate these tasks, freeing yourself up to dive into the more strategic areas of your business.

Tip: It's a good idea to batch repetitive tasks and complete them all in a single sitting. Having systems and processes in place can also show you the time-saving economies of batching specific tasks together.

Is it time to take on a team member or scale?

At some point in your business journey, you'll want to take on an employee to help you, whether that's a Virtual Assistant for a few hours a week or another full-time staff member.

When you decide to hire, you need your new team member to hit the ground running. The only way they can do that efficiently is if you can articulate what they need to do to fulfil their role. Outlining and explaining each task clearly and setting deadlines is a vital part of the process.

Tip: The easiest way to help your new team member succeed is to have business tasks written down or videos recorded as processes. It not only helps your new team member complete their tasks, but it can also mean less training and more job satisfaction.

Is there a need for more consistency in the business?

Inconsistency can breed confusion and erode trust. If your customers experience inconsistencies in your products, services, or communications, it's time to refine your systems and processes. Implementing clear guidelines and standard operating procedures ensures that everyone in your business is on the same page, delivering a consistent experience to your valued customers.

Sometimes, as your business grows, there'll be confusion or misunderstandings regarding roles, responsibilities, or tasks. If this happens, it's time to dive into your systems and processes and sort out the bumps.

Tip: Clear guidelines around your standard operating procedures, together with effective communication channels, can resolve these issues.

Do you feel overwhelmed with your never-ending to-do list?

As a small business owner, burnout is a real threat. So, if you're constantly overwhelmed and find it challenging to stay on top of your responsibilities, it's a wake-up call to assess your systems and processes.

Tip: Streamline your workflows, set priorities, and establish efficient routines to alleviate the burden of your to-do list. This might be the time to consider hiring a team and reclaim your energy.

Are costs blowing out?

Automating certain areas of your business can save you time and money. If you find your costs are blowing out, and I don't mean dollars here – I'm talking time costs, too – then it's time to consider how you can automate your business and incorporate that automation into your current systems and processes.

Tip: Consider tracking your time using an app or ask a cloud accounting expert to set up or review your existing system so that it can track areas of the business where costs are increasing. A number of cloud accounting systems can also track project time and costs too using tracking codes.

Are deadlines becoming more challenging to meet?

If you frequently encounter bottlenecks or experience delays in your operations, then it's a sign that your current systems and processes aren't working. Identify the areas where the bottlenecks occur and explore ways to streamline those processes.

Spoiler alert: The bottleneck might be you!

Tip: If you suspect that you might be the process bottleneck, write a list of all of the tasks you're currently doing yourself and look for double-ups or where you can outsource. Ask your team to help.

Are you tired of correcting mistakes?

If you've noticed a rise in errors, mistakes, or customer complaints, this could result from inefficient or inconsistent processes. When you see a pattern of recurring errors, it's time to re-evaluate and refine your systems to prevent future mistakes.

Good business is about being proactive, so invest in sound systems and processes as soon as possible. By optimising your time, enhancing productivity, and ensuring scalability, you create a strong foundation for growth and success.

Remember, by empowering yourself with efficient workflows, you'll unleash your business's potential and achieve the balance you deserve, too.

Tip: Recognise the signs that indicate improvements are needed, and take action to refine your systems and processes.

Why every business needs basic systems and processes

Systems save money. Pure and simple.

When I start working with a new client on the business finances, I first ask them to show me their cloud accounting system. More often than not, clients don't use cloud accounting at all or don't use it to its full potential. There's always a range of reasons why, but the most common one I hear is, 'I'm just a sole trader (small business owner); I can't justify the expense'.

At that point, I usually share the story of Jenny, a wonderfully creative business owner who started working with me just before the pandemic took hold in 2020.

You see, here in Australia, both the state and federal governments had a range of grant payments on offer for businesses that COVID-19 impacted. To qualify for a grant or payment, you had to meet specific criteria, such as business revenue and size, and you needed to be able to prove it.

Jenny had been working with an old-school accountant for many years. That accountant liked spreadsheets and bank statements, didn't do tech of any kind and told Jenny *not* to use cloud accounting for her business as 'it was a waste of money.' Instead, she completed complicated spreadsheets outlining revenue and expenses.

Of course, there's nothing wrong with old-school accounting. But when it came to Covid grants, spreadsheets weren't cutting it.

Spreadsheets were considered 'potentially inaccurate.' Data could be missing or easily manipulated and even if business owners provided bank statements to back up that data, governments needed to move quickly to issue funds. As such, they needed more reliable and verifiable data, ideally data from cloud accounting systems.

In this situation, business owners with no money, no customers and rejected grant applications or applications stuck in processing started to see the efficiency and value of cloud accounting. The cost was suddenly more than worth it.

Fortunately for Jenny, just before the government announced the Covid business grants and much to her accountant's chagrin, I'd convinced her of the benefits of cloud accounting. We'd set up that financial year's data retrospectively in a new cloud accounting system. And while we'll never know for sure whether or not Jenny would have ultimately received a grant producing spreadsheets as documentation, the reports from her Xero cloud accounting system definitely helped expedite the process.

Jenny has since realised all the other benefits that come with her monthly subscription, and to this day, she still tells me the system is worth every cent.

This story highlights the benefits of just one business system because we often don't look beyond the money when budgets are tight. The bottom line is that your time is valuable; there is an actual business cost for every task you manually complete, so consider what systems might save time and money and consider incorporating them into your business.

MONEY MAGNET TIP:

There are many different business systems to choose from, so it's essential to only use systems that will enhance your business and not add to the overwhelm. If it's not saving you time and money, then it's a firm no.

Basic systems for your business

If you're on the fence about adding systems to your business or need clarification on what they do or what to add, here are some to consider.

Cloud-Based Accounting Software

Example: QuickBooks Online, MYOB, Xero

There's no doubt that cloud accounting software has had the most significant impact on business finances, especially over the last five years, as AI enhancements have taken the tech from strength to strength. And while many of us are either reluctant to embrace tech or, like Jenny, don't believe it's worth the money, in my mind, as a Registered BAS Agent, it's been a game-changer. What I pay in monthly premiums, I get back a hundred times in time saved. Because my time is the most precious currency I have, that makes my cloud accounting system worth every cent.

So, what exactly is cloud accounting software?

As the name suggests, it's an online or cloud accounting system. So, cloud accounting makes your data available online when it suits you and anywhere with an internet connection.

In a nutshell, cloud accounting systems speak to your business bank account and help record income, expenses, asset purchases and any loans or liabilities your business incurs. You can access the information on multiple devices, from an iPhone to a desktop computer or tablet.

Cloud accounting systems are encrypted to ensure safety, and most now require two-factor authentication to access the data. Systems come with various features and benefits and use artificial intelligence and programming to run the engine room of your business, that behind-the-scenes data that drives financial reports.

Businesses can also run their compliance reports, interphase directly with local tax authorities, run staff wages and payments, and speak to third-party payment providers like Stripe and PayPal; heaps of automation options are designed to cut red tape and save businesses time and money.

Plus, the system allows multiple users to access the data online, so you can invite your accountant, bookkeeper and key staff members to use the program; no more relying on emails or snail-mail to complete the end-of-financial year processing.

The bottom line is that by automating bookkeeping tasks, minimising manual data entry and providing real-time financial information, cloud-based accounting software enhances efficiency and accuracy in financial management.

Project Management System

Example: Google Docs or Spreadsheet, Trello, Asana, Monday.com

A project management system allows business owners to efficiently organise and track projects, tasks, and deadlines. While a Google Document works well, digital systems like Trello, Asana or Monday.com provide a visual interface with customisable boards, lists, and cards, enabling users to assign tasks to staff or contractors, set due dates, and collaborate with team members.

A project management system lets you stay better organised, improve communication, manage projects to completion, meet deadlines and manage the workload. In my experience, setting up a project management system can be overwhelming, so this could be a good task to outsource.

Time Tracking and Invoicing System

Example: Harvest, Toggl, Clockify

Time tracking and invoicing tools can help business owners monitor their working hours, record expenses, and generate professional invoices. These systems automate the invoicing process, saving time and reducing the risk of errors. Additionally, they provide insights into billable hours, helping business owners understand the profitability of projects and allocate resources more effectively.

Digital Asset Management System

Example: Dropbox or Google Drive

Service-based and creative businesses often deal with a large volume of digital files, including images, designs, and project files. A reliable digital asset management (DAM) system, such as Dropbox or Google Drive, helps businesses securely organise, store, and share files. With advanced search functionalities and file versioning, DAM systems enhance efficiency by minimising time spent searching for specific assets, ensuring the correct files are easily accessible when needed.

Online Collaboration and Communication System

Example: Slack, Microsoft Teams, Zoom

Efficient communication and collaboration are vital for businesses with a team, especially when team members are remote or work in different locations. Platforms like Slack, Zoom or Microsoft Teams provide instant messaging, file sharing, and video conferencing capabilities, facilitating seamless communication and collaboration. These tools promote efficiency and effective teamwork by centralising discussions, sharing feedback, and eliminating unnecessary email chains.

Automated Social Media Scheduling System

Example: Hootsuite, Later, Tailwind, Meta Suite

Maintaining a solid online presence takes time and energy, and that's where social media scheduling tools are indispensable. These tools enable business owners to plan and schedule social media posts in advance across multiple platforms. By automating this process, creative entrepreneurs can save time and ensure a consistent and engaging online presence, enhancing efficiency in social media management.

Customer Relationship Management (CRM) System

Example: HubSpot, Dubsado, Salesforce

Maintaining solid relationships with clients is crucial for the success of creative businesses. A CRM system lets business owners organise customer data, track interactions, and manage leads effectively. By centralising client information and streamlining communication, CRM systems enable personalised interactions, efficient follow-ups, and improved customer satisfaction, ultimately leading to increased efficiency and business growth.

Email Marketing Platform

Example: Flodesk, Mailchimp

Email marketing software allows business owners to create, send and track email communication to their list. Using software for this process allows business owners to schedule emails in bulk ahead of time, create email nurture systems, and track and segment business leads while also showing key metrics such as open and click-through rates.

Digital Calendar

Example: Google Calendar, Outlook

Efficient time management is crucial for small business owners who must juggle multiple projects, meet deadlines, and maintain a balanced schedule. A reliable digital diary or calendar system can significantly enhance productivity, improve organisation, and increase efficiency.

Technology is pivotal in transforming businesses across all sectors in today's rapidly evolving world. Implementing suitable systems into your business can significantly enhance efficiency and productivity for small businesses.

By leveraging these systems, business owners can focus on their craft, deliver quality work, and foster long-term success in their respective industries.

MONEY MAGNET TIP:

You don't need ALL the systems on offer to run a productive and streamlined business. Instead, narrow down what you use to maximise your time and money. There is such a thing as going overboard on systems and buying every new thing on App-sumo because it makes you feel like you're taking action – but the real magic happens when to put them to good use! Finding subscriptions like Google and Microsoft 365 that perform more than one function can also be really useful. There's no one size fits all – it's all about finding the systems and processes that work for you.

Processes for increased productivity

I love a good process!

Yes, I'm that person. It just makes life easier if I have something logical to follow, especially when the creative side of my brain wants to take over and start ad-libbing. But in reality, being a stickler for good business processes helped me sell part of my business in early 2023. Why? Because the new owner didn't need to think about what to do and when, they could pick up the day they took ownership of my business, follow the processes and carry on. It meant an easy and streamlined transition for them and a better business sale price for me. If that doesn't convince you, consider the time and money you'll save on staff training, onboarding, and dealing with your business's day-to-day demands.

Business processes for the win!

Essential Processes for Small Business

Creating a great process starts with understanding what processes you need to drive your business. Once you make a list of essential processes, consider each process and document each task required to complete the process. Once you've noted each task, you can begin refining those tasks and develop a straightforward, step-by-step process that works for your business.

Once you've got the complete process written down, put the process into digital form and store all of your processes in one place. You can also create videos using a tool like Loom, for example, as you work through the process in real time. This will help your team work through each process efficiently and caters for all types of learning.

Project Management Process

Efficient project management is crucial for creative businesses to ensure smooth workflow and timely delivery. Utilising project management software, such as Trello or Asana, can help you organise tasks, set deadlines, and track progress.

For example: a designer could create a project board, assign tasks to team members, and monitor the status of ongoing projects. Project management processes increase efficiency and enhance collaboration and communication among team members.

Client Onboarding Process

Streamlining the client onboarding process creates a positive first impression, helps establish clear expectations and enhances customer satisfaction.

Develop a standardised client onboarding procedure that includes sending welcome packages, providing detailed project briefs, and setting realistic timelines.

For example: a photographer could create an automated email sequence with templates that guide clients through the booking and delivery process, addressing common questions and providing necessary information upfront and following the shoot. This process saves time, reduces confusion, and ensures a seamless client experience.

File Management Process

Effective file management is essential for small businesses, especially those dealing with a large volume of digital assets. A robust file organisation system can prevent data loss, improve accessibility, and save valuable time.

For example: a graphic designer can create a folder structure that categorises projects by client, date, or type, making it easier to locate files when needed. This organised approach minimises the risk of errors and increases efficiency in retrieving and sharing files.

Time Tracking Process

Accurate time tracking is vital for service-based business owners who often charge by the hour or need to estimate project durations. If you find time tracking a chore or have a team, you can always utilise time tracking tools like Harvest or Toggl to record time spent on different tasks and projects. This data can be invaluable for assessing project profitability, identifying productivity bottlenecks, and improving resource allocation.

For example: a virtual assistant can track the time spent on specific tasks or projects and evaluate the efficiency of their internal processes too. Tracking time can help the VA make informed decisions for future projects and pricing.

Accounting Processes (Including Invoicing and Payment Processes)

Efficient invoicing and payment processes are vital for maintaining a healthy cash flow and ensuring prompt client payment. Cloud accounting software will help you automate invoicing, generate professional-looking invoices, and send reminders for overdue payments. However, having a straightforward process for what to do and when will always ensure cash flow within the business.

For example: a podcast producer could set up recurring invoices for clients on retainer and integrate payment gateways to offer secure on-line payment options. Process-driven automation reduces administrative work, minimises errors, and accelerates the payment cycle.

It's helpful to have processes for all of the accounting functions in a business; some of these include:

- File reconciliation.

- Invoicing and payment follow-up.

- Bill receipt and payment.

- Payroll processing and payments, including superannuation.

- Month-end processing.

- Activity statement processing.

- EOFY processing.

With these processes in place, it's easier to hand off the accounting function to a team member or contract bookkeeper.

Staff Onboarding Process

You can implement several processes to help new staff transition to a valuable team member quickly and efficiently. Some of these include:

Onboarding Checklist

Develop comprehensive checklists outlining all the steps and tasks required for new employees to complete during onboarding. This checklist should include paperwork completion, orientation sessions, training modules, and introductions to key team members. By having a standardised checklist, you can ensure consistency and efficiency in onboarding each new staff member.

Welcome Package

As part of the onboarding process, prepare a welcome package that provides essential information and resources to new employees. This package may include an employee handbook, company policies and procedures, organisational charts, and other relevant materials to help them understand the business and its culture. This way, new employees can familiarise themselves with the company's values, expectations, and processes at their own pace.

Assign a Mentor or Buddy

Pairing new employees with a mentor or buddy can significantly facilitate their integration into the team and help them navigate their roles more effectively. The mentor or buddy should be an experienced team member who can provide guidance, answer questions, and offer support during the initial weeks or months. This mentorship helps new employees feel more comfortable, fosters relationships within the team, and accelerates the learning curve.

Conduct Effective Training Sessions

Efficient training sessions are essential to equip new staff members with the knowledge and skills to perform their roles effectively. Identify key topics and develop a training plan, including hands-on experience and formal instruction. Depending on the nature of your creative business, training sessions may cover software applications, design principles, photography techniques, or any other relevant areas. Consider incorporating interactive elements, such as workshops or online courses, when engaging new employees.

By implementing these essential processes, small businesses can significantly enhance their efficiency, save time, reduce costs, improve client satisfaction, and empower creative entrepreneurs to focus on what they do best.

Need help? Is it time to call in the experts?

Like many things in life, for a business to run successfully, sometimes it takes a village, especially regarding the numbers.

Whether you've been in business for years or are just starting out on your business journey, you're a sole trader or a company and no matter what your turnover, how many staff you have or what taxes you need to register for, one of the best pieces of advice I can give you is to call in the experts early, before you need them.

Now, there are lots of business experts around. But I want to speak specifically about the financial experts, what they do, and how they can help.

When I speak to business owners about the experts they use in their business, especially their financial partners, one of the common themes is that they feel uncomfortable with the person they currently employ. Sometimes, it's down to a lack of confidence, but often, they feel inferior or incompetent, and their financial partner isn't on board with their business vision or goals.

Those business owners usually want to break up with their accountant or bookkeeper but don't know how to walk away. They're afraid; don't want to be mean; are unsure of the 'unknown'; worry that there'll be repercussions; believe that maybe the accountant is right, they're crap with money and need to run their business better, or it could be due to a crazy sense of loyalty to someone who hasn't provided good service for years.

If you're reading and nodding along, consider finding someone new.

The reality is that when you hire a financial expert, you're entering into a partnership. And that partner is there to help you succeed. Sure, your financial partner might dish out some tough love now and again, but the bottom line is that it's a partnership, not a dictatorship!

You're paying someone to work with you to help you create the business you want, one that speaks to your definition of success, not something they believe or learned at university. Yep, sometimes it's not you, it's them!

So, what sort of financial partner do you need?

At the very least, every business should use a **good accountant**. Your accountant will process your end-of-year returns, provide holistic advice that considers your business and personal financial circumstances, help you set goals for your business and troubleshoot any issues you may encounter. Their expertise is in understanding all aspects of the local tax legislation related to your business and the best way to use that legislation to get you the best return at tax time.

In some cases, accountants may also process your monthly or quarterly compliance and the day-to-day bookkeeping. However, invariably, they will outsource the latter or have their staff take on this job.

In addition to hiring an accountant, a **Registered BAS Agent** can be an excellent decision for Australian-based businesses. A BAS agent can do the day-to-day bookkeeping, including payroll services.

They can also prepare and lodge your compliance obligations – Business Activity Statements (BAS), Instalment Activity Statements (IAS), Pay As You Go tax (PAYG), Single Touch Payroll, Government Grants and Taxable Payment Annual Report (TPAR). Plus, they can speak to the tax office on your behalf.

Generally, a BAS agent will be more affordable than an accountant for compliance and day-to-day bookkeeping. BAS agents can now also provide advisory services, help you set business financial goals, and offer virtual CFO services such as budgeting and cash flow forecasting. There will be an equivalent to a BAS agent in your country of residence, so it's worth checking out.

Bookkeepers provide day-to-day bookkeeping and reconciliation services and payroll and accounts payable services. They're the cloud accounting experts and often the more affordable financial professionals. Keep in mind, though, that bookkeepers cannot provide compliance or advisory services.

No matter who you choose to help with the business finances, ensure you're using a registered professional. Accountants and BAS agents must be registered with the local Tax Practitioners Board or authority, adhere to a strict code of ethics, have adequate education and insurance, and continue professional development.

So, before hiring someone new, check the local tax practitioner's website and ensure your finance professional has up-to-date registration.

MONEY MAGNET TIP:

Want to hire someone new but need help knowing where to start? Ask for recommendations because a word-of-mouth referral is often the best way to find a new finance professional. But remember, just because another business owner loves their person, it doesn't necessarily make them a good fit for you.

So, book a discovery or strategy call before making any decisions. Ask how they can help grow your business, who they currently work with and what sort of experience they have. And read their testimonials, too.

Calling in an expert when you need them will ultimately save you time and money, and financial services are a tax deduction. Think of the time you'll save outsourcing work you either don't understand or don't enjoy doing to an expert. While they're working on the books, you can work on other money-making activities requiring your expertise. If you're concerned about the cost, you can ask for fee estimates up front. Some finance professionals will offer set monthly or service fees, while others will charge an hourly rate.

Remember that your relationship with your finance professional can make a massive difference to your business. However, it only works if you enter with an open mind, share your thoughts and are prepared to implement the suggestions offered as part of the ongoing services. Like anything, if you want to see a positive change in your business, you might need to do things a little differently.

Chapter 8

Your Business Money BFFs

When it comes to business besties – aka those BFFs that tell it like it is and give you a clear strategy for what you need to do next – there's none better than the Balance Sheet and the Profit & Loss Statement (P&L)!

And before you think I've lost my mind ... yes, I know these two items are financial reports, not actual besties.

But, believe me when I tell you that these reports can give you most of the answers you need to keep your business finances in check and get a clear understanding of your business's overall financial health.

You'll find both of these reports in your cloud accounting system if you use one, and if not, your accountant can provide these reports with your end-of-year financial returns.

Ideally though, you'll have cloud accounting up and running and at the end each month dive into the Profit & Loss statement and check your net profit; but more on that later.

First: what does each report do?

MONEY MAGNET TIP:

The reports are only as good as the information you feed them, so keeping business-only bank accounts and your cloud accounting system up to date with the most accurate information is essential.

You'll also need to review your reports regularly, particularly the P&L to make the most informed decisions for your business; your financial partner can help, too.

Essential report #1: Profit and Loss Statement

The profit and loss statement, also known as the P&L, summarises the business revenue and expenses for a specific period.

Revenue includes things like:

- sales

- commissions

- payments

- licence fees

- royalties.

Expenses include both the direct costs or cost of goods sold (COGS).

They're all of the things your business requires to provide a particular service, as well as the business operating expenses or overheads.

Examples of COGS include:

- If you're a baker – it's the raw materials like flour, sugar, eggs – all the ingredients you need to make those cakes.

- If you're an interior designer or decorator and offer furniture procurement – resale items like furniture, freight, accessories would all be included.

- If you're a HR professional who specialises in hiring you might include apps or digital system costs that help to streamline the recruitment process.

- If you're a retailer your COGS will mainly consist of those whole-sale products you intend to resell.

- In some businesses COGS will include contractor and labour costs, parts, and packaging materials.

A traditional P&L highlights three separate sections of the business.

The first section: shows all of the **sales** (revenue) data and the total of those sales.

The second section: shows the **direct costs** (including COGS) and the total of those direct costs. There's also a line that shows the gross profit – the total revenue minus the total direct costs. The result is the business gross profit.

The third section: highlights all of the operating costs or overheads. Costs include fees, subscriptions, utilities, wages, superannuation, and travel, to name a few. The report then totals up all of the operating costs and reflects this total on the last line in this section.

At the bottom of the P&L statement you'll find the **all-important net profit line**. The net business profit is the gross profit minus the total operating expenses. Net profit speaks to the business's profitability and is often referred to by business owners as the 'sanity' number.

It's possible to view profit and loss statements using either cash or accrual reporting. Businesses choose one of these two accounting methods, either cash accounting and accrual accounting, when they start their business. These methods are simply two different ways to keep track of and account for the business numbers.

I explain a little more about cash or accrual accounting methods and what they mean for your business, in the glossary. You should also note that all of the numbers on the profit and loss statement still need to consider any sales taxes that you may be required to add.

Why is the P&L so important?

It's simple: the profit and loss statement gives you a snapshot of where the business money is coming from, what you're spending money on and when you're spending it.

With a single click of a button you can see business trends, peaks and troughs for sales and expenses, and that all important net profit number too, all of which will ultimately help you manage business cash flow and operations. What's not to love?

> **MONEY MAGNET TIP:**
>
> On the profit and loss statement keep an eye on:
> - The net profit number – it's worth saying again that this is the business sanity number. The net profit number will let you know if you're on track to meet your targets or not, whether the business is running at a profit (making money) or a loss (losing money).
>
> - Your revenue total – is your total revenue going up or down or are you holding steady? By monitoring your revenue total you'll get a sense of whether the business is growing, doing it tough or consistently achieving.
>
> - COGS or your direct costs and your expenses – monitoring these numbers will help you keep your spending in check. However, it's also a good way to check that what should be paid is being paid and that there are no double-ups or unexpected payments leaving the business.

Essential report #2: Balance sheet

When it comes to financial reports, the balance sheet is the one that often has business owners bamboozled. While it's a simple report per se, the confusion comes when understanding what makes up the balance sheet, how it differs from the P&L and what you can learn from it.

In simple terms, the balance sheet is a financial statement of the assets, liabilities and shareholder or business owner equity at a specific time. It's a snapshot of what the company owns and owes.

So, it's a valuable tool for business owners who want to keep a handle on that information and particularly if you ever want to sell your business.

The bottom line? A quick look at the balance sheet will tell you what your business is worth.

While it's probably not a report you'll use often, it contains valuable information and your business finance partners will use the balance sheet monthly to keep track of wages, taxes, business assets, and liabilities or to conduct an analysis of your business.

However, keep in mind that although the balance sheet reflects money in the bank, your balance sheet won't give you a sense of how sales are tracking or if your business is making a profit. You'll find this information on the profit and loss statement.

While you might be thinking that these business reports will put you to sleep or are best left to your accountant to decipher, I'd recommend taking the time to get to know these business powerhouses.

Once you know what to look for you'll be making empowered and data-driven financial decisions left and right in no time flat!

MONEY MAGNET TIP:

On the balance sheet keep an eye on:
- Your liabilities – aka what the business owes. You'll not only see what you owe on business loans and credit cards here, but also what the business owes for taxes, such as GST, VAT or sales tax, and if you have staff, on wages, staff taxes and other liabilities.

- The business equity – aka what the business is worth if you closed the doors tomorrow. Is your business value increasing or decreasing under the weight of your liabilities?

Proof is in the pudding

'Your numbers tell a story and you deserve to be the author of your story!'

Justine McLean

As a business owner, whether you choose to outsource the numbers to a specialist or DIY the business money, you must be able to read the story of your business numbers. The best way to do that is via the P&L! So, make it your mission to understand your business P&L!

Recently, I did a session inside of my Business Money Magnet™ program where we did a P&L deep-dive. As I shared with the group the topic for that day's group session, the disappointed looks told me that just about everyone on the call wished they were somewhere else. I mean a P&L deep-dive ... boring!

But, an hour later, the broad smiles told me we'd hit a chord and that I'd managed to convince the cohort just how vital understanding the P&L was to their business. I asked each member of the program to go away, read their P&L and identify a single change they could make in their business to improve the net profit.

Roll forward two weeks and the proof was definitely in the pudding:

- Melanie identified $4,500 in subscriptions costs that were no longer needed;

- James found that the offer they thought was making money was making less and costing more to deliver. They decided to refine the offer and relaunch to their subscribers.

- Barb discovered that she was losing money on the furniture procurement she offered because the correct costs were not being invoiced by the bookkeeper. Her clients were getting wholesale rates and not paying for freight so her business had lost in excess of $50K over the last six months.

- Paz realised that she was still making repayments for the printer she'd purchased even though her loan had been paid off.

- And finally, Marianne realised that her business was much more profitable than she thought and gave herself a pay increase.

These are just a few of the powerful examples of what can be uncovered when focusing your attention on your P&L and your number's story.

So, have I convinced you to make your P&L your BFF? I hope so!

Chapter 9

Budgeting for Business

At some point in your business journey, you've probably been encouraged to prepare a budget, and if not, you've no doubt heard the word budget thrown around for good measure as *the* tool that will help you save money. Whether it's a personal or business budget, when in doubt or whenever you want to do better with money, the default is the good old budget!

But here's the thing. For me, at least, budgets are a bit like diets; the idea of a reasonable budget, just like a good diet, as well as the promised outcome, can be intoxicating. You'll save money (or lose stacks of weight), so you create the budget (start the diet).

You kick it off on Monday, you're all gung-ho and feeling on top of the world, but then the weekend arrives, the temptation to spend (or eat what you shouldn't) is real. Or an unexpected cost turns up, you blow the budget (or diet), and then it goes into the too hard basket. You promise yourself you'll start over, but then it's all too hard and you're back to square one, trying to dig deep to find the motivation to start again. Or is that just me?

Despite that, I like a good budget, so at the start of each financial year, I sit down and decide what I want to earn, what I'm happy to spend and my net profit number for the year ahead. But I don't simply rely on a budget as the one single item I use in my business. And that's because, there's always a chance I won't stick strictly to my budget and I don't want to be tempted to give up on it altogether.

So instead, the budget becomes the basis for the way ahead and then I use it to decide on my overall financial goals for the year and to fill in the blanks on my cash flow forecast (there's more about cash flow in chapter 10).

Here's what you need to know about business budgets.

What is a budget?

A budget is simply a money plan. It estimates business income, what you'll earn, and business expenditure over a specific period.

Most business owners prepare a budget for 12 months, but you can set them for any period you like. Your budget helps you set money targets for your business and for business owners who are motivated by a challenge or reaching a target, a budget can be a great way to gamify your business as you strive to meet your revenue or spending goals.

For a budget to work, it needs to be purpose-driven; in other words, you need to create your budget with an end goal in mind.

For example, you might want to reach a specific revenue target, so you'll need to increase sales by a certain amount to achieve that goal.

Or, you might want to focus on reducing your costs in an endeavour to produce a better net profit result (the money left after you've paid all the bills), so over that budget period, you'll focus on expenses and have spending limits in place, for example.

> **MONEY MAGNET TIP:**
>
> The best budgets are the simple ones. So, when you create your budget choose a single outcome, for example, reduce spending or reduce spending in one specific area of the business; increase revenue by a certain percentage; have a better overall performance than the previous year. When you start with a single goal in mind, you're less likely to want to give up when the going gets tough.

Essential elements of a good budget

If you've decided to go down the budget route, you should make it the best budget possible, so here are the things you should consider as you prepare your budget.

- What's your time frame? Most budgets are usually twelve months or for a full financial year. However, you can create monthly or quarterly budgets.

- Consider your fixed costs and add them in from the start – these are expenses that are unlikely to change in the short term, for example, rent, salaries, loan repayments or leasing or insurance costs.

- What are the variable costs? These are the expenses that fluctuate and include utilities, materials, staff costs if you hire subcontractors or casuals, subscriptions and other overheads. These can also include unexpected costs like repairs.

- What turnover or revenue target will you include? The revenue target can be a tricky element in any budget, so, to keep it simple, look at the prior year's revenue and devise an income estimate using that figure. If your business has been running for a while, you'll likely see where the peaks and troughs are in your business and can build these into your new budget. You should also consider new initiatives, products or services that might be on the horizon, respective launch dates and what impact you expect them to have on the turnover.

- Consider tax savings and other staff costs like leave accruals, superannuation or insurance. If you plan to hire new staff, anticipate the new hire costs and add these to the budget, too.

Creating your tailored business budget

1. Decide on your business financial goals for the budget period. If you're putting together a budget for the next 12 months, decide where you want your business to be financially 12 months from now.

2. Download a blank budget template from your cloud accounting software programme. If you don't use cloud accounting, most federal or state government business sites will have budget templates.

3. Decide on a timeframe for your budget – there are no hard and fast rules here, but because creating a budget can be time consuming, most business owners will create a budget for 12 months.

4. There's a lot of benefit in reviewing what's already happened in your business and using that data to create a new budget. So grab a copy of the profit and loss statement for the last 12 months and look at the actual totals for each income and expense item in the business and use those numbers as a starting point.

Now it's time to consider what stays in the budget and what goes.

For example: there might be a service you're no longer offering or an expense that was a one off. In each case, these items no longer need to be factored into your budget.

This part of the budgeting process can be completed quite quickly but if you want to do an overhaul of your income and expenses, just don't get so bogged down that you give up.

It's often easier to keep it as simple as possible at this stage, decide on the income and expense lines you'll need for the next 12 months and do an expense deep-dive, for example, at a later stage.

5. Once you know the income and expenses that stay and those that go, you can approach this next stage of the budgeting task in two ways.

The simple budget – in the spirit of keeping it simple, the easiest way to complete your budget is to add a blanket percentage increase or decrease across the board.

For example: you could add five or ten percent to the previous year's revenue total to generate your budgeted revenue for the year ahead. Or, incorporate a two or three-percent decrease on the previous year's actual expenditure to come up with your expense budget targets.

Another way to create a simple budget is to look at the total of each income and expense line for the previous 12 months and decide to rinse and repeat over the next 12 months. In other words, your targets remain unchanged. In this case, you can divide the total of the previous year's income and expenses by 12 and plot these into each month of the budget or adjust the numbers for seasonal variances.

The not so simple budget – I'm reluctant to use the word complex because I don't want to put you off. But, if you want a more accurate budget or you've got a little more time to devote to budget preparation, you can always take each income line and each expense line and make an individual decision on your targets for the year ahead.

For example: If you offer five different services but know you'll only focus on promoting one of those over the next 12 months, you might like to set a bigger income target for the promoted service and a more modest revenue budget for the other services.

While it's not a more complicated approach to budgeting, it will take more time to finalise your budget.

6. Now it's time to enter the data into your budget template, or if you have cloud accounting software, you can enter each line item directly into your software.

Once that's done, you can 'play' with the numbers to give you the outcome you're after.

For Example: You enter the budget you've decided on but then realise these numbers give you a budget deficit or loss and you're not going to reach your targets. In this case you can go back to the drawing board and decrease your expenses or increase your revenue to make the numbers work.

The bottom line is that this exercise is more than just pulling numbers from the air. It's about analysing whether the budget you've decided will give you the desired outcome and is something achievable.

> **MONEY MAGNET TIP:**
>
> Even if you aren't creating a budget, step four above is a great exercise to undertake when you want to save money. By checking each line on your P&L, you can flag obsolete expenses or see areas where you're doubling up on costs or could reduce your spending.

You've done your budget. What next?

It's all about the analysis!

There's no point going to all the trouble of creating a budget unless you plan on spending the time analysing the actual numbers vs the budget. In other words, what really happened in your business, -what was the actual revenue you earned and how did this stack up against your budgeted number and your goal or what did you actually spend vs your planned spending?

You can do a budget analysis using your cloud accounting software, it's as simple as running a report, or alternately with some good, old-fashioned maths.

A monthly budget check should form part of your business money to-do list and you can incorporate this into your Money Monday date once a month.

Here are some things you'll be able to tell from your budget analysis:

You're overspending.

If that's the case ask yourself:

- Where can you cut costs and save money?

- Is it time for a spending freeze?

Your revenue has room to improve.

If that's the case:

- Identify the non-performing products and services, then consider what services you need to revamp or what products or services you can eliminate.

- Is it time to increase your prices? If it's been more than 12 months since you've reviewed prices, it's a good time to review.

- Do you need to find new revenue sources? Where can your business diversify?

You've got extra funds in the coffers!

If that's the case:

You can then consider the best way to use the additional money, for example: depositing some money in a rainy day account.

- Think about using the money to reduce your debt.

- Is it time to scale your business – add new staff, for example or invest in new tech or buy new capital?

- You might consider giving yourself a pay increase?

Creating a business budget will take time and effort. But when used consistently, it can be a great tool to help you achieve your business's financial goals.

But, as I mentioned at the outset, budgets are a bit like diets because often, when we muck them up or aren't consistent with the analysis, we give up. So, before you dive in, consider if a budget is really for you.

Mark's story

Mark, a talented creative director, was an over spender – it was the first thing he shared with me when we sat down in our first meeting about his business.

Over many years in business he felt he'd wasted tens of thousands of dollars on impulse buys and by simply not paying any attention to his expenses.

When I first suggested that we create a budget for Mark's business, he was horrified. He felt there was *no way* he would stick to it and it was essentially a waste of time and money. Nevertheless, I managed to convince him to give it a try.

We sat together and started with a full expense review, working out what expenses stayed and what needed to go. Once we'd done that, we set a realistic spending limit each month and using a bit of a 'Profit First' hybrid, decided on what percentage of his revenue we would allocate to the business expenses. This allocation would cover off the budgeted expenses over the year.

Now, before I continue, if you're wondering what *Profit First* means, it's essentially a system pioneered by Mike Michalowicz where every time you get a deposit from a sale in your business you allocate a predetermined percentage of that money to wages, expenses and profit.

To facilitate the expense allocation, Mark set up a new bank account and called it expenses. You'll recall that in my simple approach to business bank accounts all sales go into and all expenses come out of a single operating account. However, Mark didn't trust himself to use the operating account to pay the bills, deciding that if he saw a large balance, he'd be tempted to spend the money. So, expense account to the rescue!

From then on, each and every time Mark made a sale, he would go into his operating account and transfer 30 percent of that sale to his expense bank account. When it came time to pay the bills, he was on strict instructions to only use what was in the expense account to make those payments. Under no circumstances was Mark allowed to dip into the operating account for extra funds.

Additionally, we made sure that Mark received his wages each week, also as a transfer from the operating account.

While it took patience and there were more than a few hiccups and slips along the way, after five months, the new system and regularly referring to the budget became second nature for Mark. He was able to get his spending on track but more than that, he decided to budget an ambitious revenue target for the year and found that the regular budget check-in was all the motivation he needed to meet his targets.

When it comes to budgets, Mark is now one of the biggest cheerleaders for the positive impact they can make on both business and money mindset too.

Chapter 10

It's All About Cash Flow!

You don't have to be in business for very long to know that cash is the all-important business currency and that consistent cash flow is the *only* thing that matters! When you've got nothing in the bank, your bills don't get paid, your wages don't get paid, and unless you rely on personal savings, your business will grind to a halt!

I love a good cash flow forecast! It's the number one tool I use in my business and in my opinion, a far more helpful tool than a budget. And, if you're a business with lumpy income, in other words, you don't have regular income but instead rely on big launches, finalising large projects before you get paid, or client flow is uncertain, then a cash flow is a must for your business too!

Good business is all about good cash flow!

And good cash flow begins with a forecast.

In its simplest form, a cash flow forecast is a measure of the money coming into and going out of your business.

For most businesses, the cash flowing in comes from selling products or services. However, cash could also flow into the business through refunds, loans, grants, interest, rebates, commissions, referrals and licence fees.

Cash outflows include all operating expenses, the cost of sales (COGS or direct costs), salaries and wages, and things like loan repayments, superannuation and tax liabilities.

A favourable cash flow position is vital for a business to remain profitable and successful. That's why creating a system to track business cash flow, known as a cash flow forecast, can help business owners with the peaks and troughs that inevitably come along in the business journey.

Unlike a budget, which speculates what your business might earn and what you might need to spend, a cash flow forecast is based mainly on actuals: actual sales and actual expenses. As a result, creating a cash flow forecast is pretty straightforward, as it's based on data you have ready access to.

You can create a cash flow forecast at any time and for any period, and a spreadsheet is one of the best ways to get it down on paper. You should monitor it regularly; I look at mine weekly.

A good cash flow forecast is really empowering – it means you'll know when it's okay to spend money in your business. You'll also see when you must save for months when the cash flow could improve.

How to create a cash flow forecast

1. First off, grab a copy of a cash flow forecasting template. If you'd like the link to the template I use in my business, check out the book resources page: https://www.justinemclean.com/book-re sources.

2. Start with a 90-day forecast of incoming revenue and outgoing expenses.

3. Choose the day and date from which you'll start your cash flow forecast, open the spreadsheet, and add the start date. I always start at the beginning of a month because starting there makes life easy. While you can create a daily or weekly forecast, I recommend a monthly forecast as the best practice.

4. Add the opening bank balance. At the top of my template, you'll see an area to add your opening bank balance, but all good cash flow forecasts should have a space for this. The opening balance is usually the balance of your business bank account at the end of the previous day.

5. Review your sales figures from last financial year. These will not only provide a jumping-off point in estimating projected sales targets for the period ahead but can also highlight the peaks and troughs for sales and where you might need to make adjustments. Forecasting future sales may land in the too-hard basket for many business owners, as it's like looking into a crystal ball, but previous sales figures are a great basis from which to make your best guess at projected sales.

   I recommend going back into this part of the spreadsheet weekly, or at the very least monthly and updating the forecast with your actual sales figures once a period has ended. For example: on 1 April you could update the sales figures for March using the actual revenue received. In this case, your March figures will flow through on the forecast and provide more accurate data on your cash flow position in the months ahead.

6. Factor in sales. Most businesses will receive the bulk of their cash inflow from sales. However, other non-sales income may come into your business in the year ahead. So, when preparing your cash flow forecast, also consider:

- Are you likely to receive any tax refunds?
- Are there any business grants you've applied for, which you could consider adding those into the cash inflow area of the forecast?
- Do you have capital coming into the business from investors?
- Will you receive any royalties, commissions or licence fees?

7. Factor in your expenses. Hopefully, you have a clear idea of when the business bills are due and the amount of those regular expenses; you can add the costs you know about into the cash outflows area of the forecast template.

   You can update this area as each new bill arrives. Include all of your business expenses in this section.

   Some examples include:

   - rent
   - marketing and office expenses
   - vehicle expenses
   - bank fees and charges
   - salaries and contractor fees
   - superannuation payments for staff and yourself
   - loan or interest repayments
   - tax bills
   - dividends
   - new planned asset purchases
   - upgrades to tech or business systems.

As you receive actual bills, dive back into the forecast and update the spreadsheet.

I gather all my bills and do this as part of my Finance Friday routine.

> **MONEY MAGNET TIP:**
>
> Creating a cashflow forecast is not going to be a perfect science. Of course, if you know you have a significant launch or a new product offering in a particular month, you can adjust your revenue projections accordingly. Likewise, if you intend to increase prices, include your forecasts based on the price increase.
>
> Also, keep in mind when you expect to receive payments. It's one thing to include likely sales, but if your clients are slow payers, consider the date you think you'll receive the income rather than the date you invoice.

How to improve your cash flow

The cash flow forecast is ready once the opening balances and the projected revenue and expenses are in place. Next, it's time to review the projected net balance of the business each month to determine your cash flow position.

Doing this will allow you to highlight those months ahead when cash flow is poor or where you need to save for the bigger expenses, like tax time. It also allows you to see where there's an opportunity to save additional funds or make capital purchases, for example.

But this is not a 'set and forget' exercise. No matter what stage of business you're in, getting really clear on your cash flow allows you to move forward with clarity and confidence. For instance, if you're in a negative cash flow position or the money is starting to get tight, it's a good idea to get proactive and work out ways to bring in more money or cut costs before you land in dire straits. Improving cash flow early in the process can save heartache when that significant tax bill lands or an opportunity arises that needs cash input.

To improve your cash flow, a great place to start is to review and update your invoicing procedures.

It always surprises me how many business owners delay creating and sending their invoices. Incorporating good invoicing practices into your business is vital to keep the cash flowing.

Here are some invoicing strategies to consider:

- Invoice as soon as the job is complete. Better still, if you're a service provider, ask for a service deposit of up to 50%, take progress payments or full payment upfront.

- Shorten your invoice terms or encourage your customers to pay early by giving them a small discount.

- Make it easy for your customers to pay you. Consider third-party payment services like Stripe so customers have the convenience of paying with a credit card, for example.

- Chase up late payers. If you'd prefer a separation between yourself as the business owner and the client, set up an 'accounts' department and an accounts email address.

  Whether you have an accounts department or not, chasing up late payments this way makes your business seem larger than it is and allows someone else, albeit a fictitious someone, to be the 'bad guy' chasing payments.

- Identify your biggest costs and find ways to save.

> **MONEY MAGNET TIP:**
>
> Do you know what it costs you to run your business? If you don't know, it's time to find out!
>
> One of the additional benefits of a cash flow forecast is that you'll have to keep track of your monthly expenses so your 'cost of doing business number' (CODB) will always be top of mind.
>
> Once you know your CODB, keeping track of business costs and cutting where needed is a sure fire strategy to increase cash flow.

How to reduce costs and save money in your business

Negotiate the direct costs (COGS) with your suppliers: When it comes to business costs, there's always room for improvement. So, take a critical look at your direct costs; are they all non-negotiable? Can you save money by improving processes or introducing tech?

Talk to your suppliers and determine how they can help you or how you can help each other.

Can you:

- Negotiate longer payment terms?

- Pay up front and get a better deal?

- Return stock that isn't selling?

- Get a discount on your next order to bring in new items with a faster turnover?

- Ask for better terms on bulk orders or freight charges?

- Buy end of line items at a clearance price to give you a higher profit margin?

- Cancel automatic backorders when your cash flow can't afford new items?

- Consider a service swap and trade services with a key supplier to save some money?

Reduce operating costs: Operating costs may be vital to running your business, so when you need to cut costs, the best place to start is with the overheads or operating expenses. Look for ways to reduce overhead costs, particularly subscriptions (see chapter 14), such as rent, utilities, and insurance, by negotiating with suppliers, finding more energy-efficient solutions, and shopping around for more cost-effective solutions. There are many online comparison sites, but often, the easiest way to negotiate a better deal is to jump on a call and speak directly to your supplier.

Reduce marketing costs: Instead of outsourcing your marketing and PR, focus on low-cost marketing methods. Consider email marketing and social media to reach customers and reduce advertising expenses. Think about connection, collaboration, local area marketing and whom you can work with in mutually beneficial ways for your business.

If you use Google or Facebook ads, analyse the results regularly and eliminate campaigns that are delivering high-cost or few leads.

Outsource non-core activities: As the business owner and most likely the face of the business, you'll have a cache that is integral to your business's success. Most business owners know their product or service better than anyone else, so it makes sense for them to spend their time working on revenue generation. However, many business owners try to be everything to their business; they want to do *all* the jobs, no matter how mundane.

So, look at all the activities that go into running your business and call in the experts in accounting, IT or admin. They might cost money now, but the time saving will be worthwhile in the long run.

Reduce rent: If you're renting, speak to your landlord about your lease. Is there room for a rent reduction in exchange for a longer lease term, for example? Another way to save when you're renting is to speak to the landlord about rental outgoings. These costs can often be a drain on cash flow so talk to your landlord about ways to save on the outgoings. Suggest that they negotiate better deals with suppliers to help you save. And, if ever you're struggling with rental payments, reach out about longer payment terms or ask about the opportunity to sublease your premises, space permitting.

Review insurances and utilities annually: where can you get better deals and discounts? This can be an opportunity to save significant amounts and you should do an annual review.

Streamline operations: Where can you improve systems and process-es, eliminate inefficiencies or add tech to help the business save time and money? Your staff are often your best asset when it comes to finding efficiencies within your business, so speak to your team about the day-to-day processes and get their input around improving business systems.

It's also worth analysing business IT costs. Do you hire an IT expert on retainer, for example, and if so, are you utilising their services efficiently. Also, look at day-to-day business emails. Rather than creating a new email address for each new staff member, consider generic email ad-dresses like admin@ or sales@ to save money and time.

Talk to an expert: When it comes to tech and systems, we often end up with overlaps, or worse, we don't take full advantage of the tech systems we have in place. As part of implementing automation and technology solutions, consider hiring an expert to guide you. It might cost more money at the outset, but it can save you money in the long term.

Labour costs: Staff and related staffing costs can significantly burden business, so consider flexible working arrangements for your staff if employment contracts allow. This could mean employing people on a part-time, casual or freelance basis or a hybrid of WFH and coming into the office. Consider outsourcing to a contractor rather than a new hire.

Reduce waste: Does your business have a waste problem? If so, what are you wasting: time, money, resources or all of the above? Look at all areas of the business and make an effort to reduce waste. Implement recycling, review systems and operations, and look at each job position for efficiencies and cost savings.

Get smart with tech: There's no doubt that using technology and incorporating smart systems into your business can save time and money. However, if you want tech to be a real money saver, you have to use it to its full potential. So, take some time and review the tech you're currently using – where can you improve or find efficiency? Often the best way to do this is to ask an expert, someone who understands how to make the most of the tech you're currently using and can suggest ways to help your best utilise it to its maximum potential.

Other things to consider when it comes to saving money with tech:

- How are the systems and tech you're currently using helping to improve business performance? Where are you doubling up? Do you need to consolidate systems? Can you downgrade to a cheaper or free version?

- Using email in your business – consider generic emails like admin@ or help@ where you're using multiple staff or there could be high staff turnover.

- Look at AI for your business and how it can help. From Chat GPT to Midjourney, Claude to Chatbots and Zapier to Xero cloud-based accounting – there are so many systems already using artificial intelligence to improve efficiency and help workflow as well as dedicated AI alternatives for everything from writing content to creating imagery. It's worth investigating how these can help your business and save time and money in the process.

- And if you're not sure how artificial intelligence can help in your business and don't have time to do the research, ask AI, like ChatGPT, for example, how AI can help your business improve and grow now and into the future.

Do you incentivise your staff?

Your team, no matter how big or small, is one of the most important assets in your business. So, next time you need a cash boost, ask your team for help to determine ways to increase sales, improve productivity or cut costs. Offer them bonus commissions or other performance incentives where measurable improvement has occurred.

No matter how long you've been in business or how experienced you are, a lack of cash can mean the end of your business, so if you do nothing else when it comes to the business money, keeping a regular eye on the cash flow will be the biggest game changer of all in your business.

A story about cash flow and lumpy income

Gerri runs a business that uses a live-launch formula. In other words, the business opens up an opportunity to join the coaching program on offer, but only does this for one week at a time, four or five times a year. Essentially there are four or five big paydays and for the other weeks in the year – those non-launch weeks – Gerri doesn't make a cent.

Now, before you get too worried about Gerri's wellbeing, it's worth pointing out that Gerri's business turns over in excess of one million dollars a year and she makes a good profit too, so there's definitely money in the bank to live on and to help run the business. Well, most of the time!

When Gerri started working with me, there were a couple of big issues we needed to address and overcome. Gerri kicked off our first meeting and said, 'my business is making no money, I don't think we'll survive'. Of course, when I reviewed the profit and loss statement, what I saw told a very different story. The first thing I noticed was that Gerri raked in the dough, albeit with only four or five paydays a year. However, as fast as it was coming in, it was also going out. Wages and expenditure was high and the bank account had only a few hundred dollars in it. There were no savings of any kind. Cash flow was an issue.

It's no wonder that Gerri had developed a feast or famine mentality when it came to her business and genuinely thought her business was about to go bust. While there was always another opportunity for a large payday on the horizon, with no cash flow and no guaranteed income, the business was in real trouble.

Luckily, there was plenty we could do – and here's what we did next:

1. The biggest priority was to get a cash flow in place. Determine what was coming in, but more importantly, what was going out.

2. Next, we took a deep dive into the expenses and quickly realised that the business couldn't afford the very large salary Gerri was taking for herself. That pill was a hard one to swallow.

3. We then approached various suppliers and asked for discounts and longer payment terms. Following this process, we got rid of almost $50K in non-essential expenses.

4. Once the cash flow forecast was updated with Gerri's new salary

and the revised expenses, we ran a highlighter through those months when large expenses were due, particularly those quarterly payments to the tax office. That gave us a basis for a savings plan, not only for the taxes, but also for the rainy day account which we'd opened.

5. Next, we looked at future launch dates and diarised the key payments that the business had to set aside from the revenue collected. This was money that would cover future expenses.

6. Gerri also set up a new direct debit for her salary and superannuation payments and made a commitment to wait until 'payday' each week for spending money; no more dipping into the business account and taking 'just a little bit extra'!

7. Once we'd done all of that, we took a look at Gerri's offers to see if there was anything the business could offer in evergreen or for purchase at any time to provide an additional source of income. We also investigated adding other income streams that might be suitable for the business.

8. Finally, we looked at the live-launch model and decided to test run giving prospective clients payment options when they joined. As it turned out, giving clients the option of progress payments meant that more clients joined the program, and Gerri and the business also had regular monthly income to look forward to rather than four or five big lump sums.

We attacked it from a few different angles, to create massive success. Not only did our action plan significantly improve the cash flow in the business, but after some work, Gerri's mindset around her business and revenue improved too.

The result, despite the business still having lumpy income, is that Gerri now feels comfortable about how to manage her business and is confident of continued success. She also now saves for her taxes and has a great rainy day account balance, so she knows that if the next launch is a flop, both her and the business will be okay.

Chapter 11

Compliance – A Necessary Evil?

You've undoubtedly heard about business compliance at some point on your business journey. This very unsexy term refers to those legal, regulatory, ethical and tax requirements at both state and federal levels that you may have to adhere to or register for, to ensure your business meets its obligations and operating standards.

To operate legally and ethically, you must meet all compliance obligations related to your business, location and industry. And while you might be tempted to skip this chapter altogether (even I think compliance is a little boring) it's one of those business necessary evils. Therefore, I'd encourage you to take a deep breath and read on because at some point in your business journey, you'll need to understand your obligations.

No matter where you operate a business, like it or not, you'll be expected to follow specific compliance obligations. These obligations vary depending on the type of business you operate, your business structure, location and annual turnover.

This area of business can be confusing and getting your head around all the laws, regulations and requirements is enough to make anyone's head spin. I mean, who started their business to spend time crossing the T's and dotting the I's? However, failure to comply with mandatory obligations can result in fines, penalties and, in some cases, legal action. So, if in doubt, *always, always* consult the experts. Believe me, this is not the place to start guessing.

You can always ask a business or financial expert to set up your business for compliance and even manage any day-to-day compliance tasks on your behalf – often at great expense. However, no matter how time-consuming, complicated or confusing, all business owners have a duty of care to themselves and their business to understand their ongoing compliance obligations, key dates, financial liability and who to turn to, to ask for help.

While staying up to date with any changes in legislation that can impact your business or industry is also essential, my recommendation is to call on the experts when in any doubt. Ask your financial partner to let you know when things change, how these updates will impact your business and what steps you need to take to remain compliant.

What you might need to sign up for?

Here are some examples of business compliance. This list is not exhaustive, and there will be specific information relating to your country/state, so check with your local authority or business expert.

- **Business registration**: Involves registering your business name and identifier with the appropriate government agencies.

  For example: In Australia, anyone running a business will need a business identifier, aka an ABN (Australian Business Number). This is a unique eleven-digit number and national identifier which you can apply for via the business.gov.au website. You may also want to register for a business name and this registration is done through ASIC and is a national registration.

- **Business taxes**: Depending on where you operate and your business type, you may have several business tax liabilities. These taxes are mandatory and will be automatically applied following tax processing time, whether annually, quarterly, monthly or more frequently. In some cases, you will be liable for both federal and state taxes.

  However, depending on your business's size, turnover and structure, you must register for some taxes.

  For example: In Australia, you must register for Goods and Services Tax (GST) once your business turnover reaches $75,000 (in a financial year).

  As the tax side of business is complicated and ever-changing, please check with your local tax advisor as soon as possible so you're aware of what taxes you might be liable to pay as part of running your business.

- **Labour laws**: If you're employing staff or contractors, you'll need to know a lot of information to ensure you comply with your employer's obligations. From minimum pay and conditions to occupational health and safety requirements (OHS), taxes, insurance and leave obligations. Again, these may vary from state to state and there may be federal laws in addition to state laws.

- **Data privacy**: Running a business and working with clients and staff means that, at some point, you'll have access to personal information. You'll be required to protect that information according to the relevant legislation in your region. Know what you need to do to protect information but also understand what to do in case of a data breach or requirements for destroying information that's no longer required.

- **Environmental protection**: Ecological laws may cover the land, water and air where you operate, so understand how these might impact you and your business. There may also be noise pollution and waste management requirements that apply to your business.

- **Business insurance**: There are various types of insurance you should have in place when running a business and it's vital to understand where you need to be covered. From workers' compensation to accident and liability insurance, product liability, and professional liability, the list goes on! Consult an insurance broker to ensure you're covered, and review your insurance needs yearly.

- **Permits and licences:** You will be required to do certain activities in your business, so check with your local authorities what you might need.

Other things to consider include copyright, trademark and intellectual property. But speaking to an expert and determining your compliance obligations from the get-go is best!

MONEY MAGNET TIP:

With any sort of compliance, there will be reporting requirements, too. Yep, there's no avoiding the paperwork! So, note critical dates and know when things are due.

Record keeping like a pro

As part of maintaining compliance in your business you'll need to understand what record keeping protocols to maintain and what supporting documentation you need to have in place to give to authorities if re-quired.

In most jurisdictions, you are legally required to keep records of all trans-actions that relate to your staff, taxation, superannuation, registrations and any documents that relate to your business's income and expenses.

The good news here is that if you use cloud accounting, most of the heavy lifting in record keeping compliance is done as these systems not only keep a record of all transactions, but in some cases, you're also able to attach documentation to transactions and store documentation, too.

In general, you must keep all records for a period of five years. However, this may change depending on where you operate your business. So, once again, it's best to check with your business expert or local authority to ensure you've got this final piece of the puzzle in hand.

When I think about record keeping, I always think of my client Dave.

Dave is a photographer and so his business is equipment heavy. There's always a new gadget, or a new lens to add to the arsenal. But Dave also had a habit of losing things and breaking things, and so the big expenses in his business, aside from buying new equipment, were the repairs and replacement costs.

We had an equipment hire line built into every job to ensure we were banking money for the inevitable lost and damaged equipment but it felt like every week there was a new purchase or another insurance claim to process. But, when I started working with Dave, although he paid a huge insurance premium every year for loss and damage to equipment, he'd never made a claim. When I asked him why, he said it was because he'd never kept the paperwork and so had no proof of purchase.

So, we immediately went back through all the recent purchases and got hold of the paperwork. Once we had that information, we digitised it, kept a copy on a local server and then put another copy into Xero (Dave's cloud accounting software). While this was an overwhelming task at the beginning, once everything was loaded, it became second nature each time a purchase was made.

And this simple task of keeping purchase records had so many benefits.

First, we could make insurance claims when things got lost or damaged.

But, we also had all of the purchase details and records in one place so Dave's accountant found it easy to prepare the depreciation portion of the company tax return. And years later when the tax office audited Dave, he had all of his invoices in one place and could prove his expenditure. I'd say that was a win-win-win and a great reason to keep good records too.

Commit to saving for compliance

Have you ever had that heart-sinking feeling when the tax bill arrives and you realise there's not enough money in the bank to pay for it? I've been there, and honestly, I don't recommend putting yourself in that position. Ever!

So, once you know what compliance you're liable for in your business, one of the best business money habits I can encourage you to adopt is committing to saving for the business compliance expenses.

Compliance obligations are usually due at the same time every quarter or year, so step one is to make a list of compliance due dates and put those into your calendar. Then, it's all about a savings plan.

When it comes to saving for compliance, particularly tax, many questions seem to stop us before we even start – what's the right amount to put aside? What should you do with the savings? How often should you save?

But, saving for compliance can be pretty simple because it's all about discipline and consistency, even when times are tough.

Here are some tips to help you save for compliance:

1. Open a tax savings or compliance account (if you haven't already) and keep all your money for compliance in one place. Go for a fee-free, linked account that doesn't have a debit card attached. Give your account a name so that you remind yourself to save for compliance every time you see it.

2. Be consistent. Make regular deposits and monitor your compliance account monthly. Compare your compliance account balance with your business compliance reports. If you've got enough funds in the account, great; if not, transfer extra to cover your compliance. Once you've paid your compliance obligations, if you have funds left in your savings account, you can use these towards personal tax or staff bonuses or reinvest the money into the business.

3. If consistency is an issue, or you're time-poor, set up direct debits, pick a nominal amount based on previous returns and set up a regular transfer. If you're worried about cash flow, break it down into a weekly amount to help with consistency. If you need help with what to save, ask your tax advisor to help.

4. Once the money is transferred safely to your compliance savings account, it's no longer yours! Act as if you've given the money away; hopefully, you won't be tempted to redraw those savings. When you're consistently saving money for compliance, you'll no longer have to worry about finding the money when paying your compliance bills and that's definitely worth the effort.

Top tips to save consistently

- **Transfer an amount for any sales tax, VAT or GST you collect when it arrives.**

  For example: My business is registered for GST, so I need to give 10 percent of everything I earn to the government. To stay on top of my GST compliance and to make my life simple, I transfer 10% of everything I earn to my tax savings account at the end of every week. Sure, it's overkill, but it means I'll always have enough at tax time and a little extra, too.

- **Transfer any payroll taxes and superannuation amounts due the same day you run the payroll.**

  In most cases, your staff taxes won't be due until some time in the future, but with so many pulls on business cash flow, it's better to have the money you owe for this compliance safely saved rather than trying to find it when it's due. I say out of sight, out of mind!

- **Refer to previous years as a guide.**

  Need to pay company tax or other taxes but need to figure out your liability? Look at what you paid for that particular tax in the previous period and save a similar amount.

Business Foundation checklist

☐ *I know my:*

- business structure

- business compliance and registration obligations

- accounting status – cash or accrual.

☐ *Business bank accounts set up for:*

- day-to-day operations

- tax savings

- rainy day or profit savings

- business credit card.

☐ *I've got the right experts on my team.*

Some suggestions:

- Accountant

- Bookkeeper

- Coach

- VA

- Social Media Manager

- Web Developer.

☐ *Cloud accounting is up and running.*

☐ *Training in the cloud accounting basics organised.*

☐ *Business systems and processes in place.*

☐ *Best practice invoicing in place.*

☐ *Success definition for the next period completed.*

☐ *Financial goal set!*

☐ *Budget set up.*

☐ *Cost of doing business completed.*

Here are some expenses to review regularly:

- contractor fees, wages and salaries

- rent

- utilities

- marketing and advertising costs

- subscriptions

- supplies and materials required to deliver your products and services

- tech costs – subscriptions and contractors

- insurance

- travel

- entertainment.

☐ *Personal expenses reviewed – what wage is required to sustain your lifestyle.*

☐ *Cashflow forecast set up.*

☐ *Expenses reviewed – look for savings.*

☐ *Profitable pricing calculated.*

☐ *Website and assets updated.*

☐ *Clients advised.*

☐ *Ascension model / value ladder reviewed and in place with new pricing.*

☐ *Weekly Money Monday or Finance Friday in the calendar.*

☐ *Baseline numbers to track noted and ready for review.*

☐ *Savings plans set up for:*

- compliance

- rainy day.

☐ *Time set aside to work on my money story or to meditate.*

☐ *Quarterly review and goal-setting sessions in the calendar!*

Money Magnet

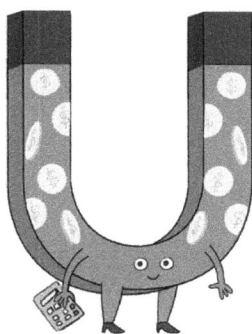

Chapter 12

Profitable Pricing Formula

'Pricing is my superpower! Give me 90 minutes and your numbers, and I'll give you a profitable pricing strategy every single time.'

Justine McLean

That quote was a throwaway line at a photo shoot a few years back, which soon became the rallying cry for my business.

Pricing, particularly pricing for profit, was one of those areas of business *all* my clients struggled with. Over the years, I've also found it a struggle, particularly as I changed my business model, my skills increased or my money story got the better of me.

Why?

Well, for most business owners – me included – pricing can be a mish-mash of confusing elements, all of which takes centre stage at some point: expectation, mindset, self-worth, woo-woo and then, of course, all of those practicalities that go into pricing.

There have also been a lot of pricing 'experts' around, sharing conflicting information about the best way to come up with your pricing structure, so I could see why the pricing was, and in a lot of cases, still is one of those set-and-forget, overwhelming, or wholly ignored areas of business.

That said, as I soon discovered, creating a pricing structure that is both profitable and easy to follow is crucial for business success and bringing in the sort of money both I and my clients are in business to earn. So, my self-imposed mission became to devise a way to price products and services that didn't involve second-guessing, comparison, meditation or woo-woo – and that put self-doubt and all those inevitable money stories we tell ourselves firmly in the corner. And that's how I created my Profitable Pricing Formula.

MONEY MAGNET TIP:

Make pricing a breeze, head to https://www.justinemclean.com/book-resources and checkout the Profitable Pricing Formula mini-course.

Pricing for Profit!

In today's competitive market, setting the right price for your products or services is crucial for the success of your business. Before you decide on your prices, you must clearly define what 'success' looks like for you in this business season because your prices should be tied directly to your definition of success and goals.

However, the perfect pricing strategy should also maximise your profits and help you attract more ideal customers, which is where my Profitable Pricing Formula can help.

But before I share the exact system I've been using for years to help you uncover your profitable pricing, I want to ask you a question.

When it comes to pricing your services and products, on a scale of 1 to 10, how do you feel?

- **10** – you're confident, it's no problem!

- **6-9** – you review your prices regularly, every year or two, and feel pretty good about where you're sitting.

- **5** – you think you've got it, but every time you set your prices, self-doubt kicks in, and you backtrack and do nothing.

- **2-4** – I've thought about making a change but get overwhelmed; it's all just too hard!

- **1** – you set your prices once upon a time when you started your business and haven't looked at them since.

When I start working with new clients, I always ask this question, particularly when they tell me their pricing needs a review. In all my years in business, not a single business owner has ever given themselves a score over 5. Hopefully, you'll be the exception!

Naturally, I ask why they feel uncertain about their prices, and it usually comes back to a lack of self-worth or comparison. In most cases, there's concern about what everyone else is charging and how their business fits into the overall picture; they don't want their prices to be too low or too high; just right will do, so they choose prices somewhere in the middle regardless of the type of business they're running or what it costs them to run their business. Or worse, lack of self-worth means they gravitate to charging the same price as the cheapest service provider, sometimes even less.

Either way, whether you're undercutting everyone else, charging the same prices, or somewhere in the middle, you need to understand your business circumstances to avoid setting yourself up to fail or ending up in a race to the bottom, because no one wants that!

One thing I know for sure, though, is that after all my years in business, none of my clients start out wanting to charge top dollar or more than everyone else in their industry. Why? Because there's a mindset issue around charging top dollar. It's seen as showing off or big-noting, and why would they want to do that' or in some cases, my clients don't believe they deserve or are worth the money.

I want that attitude to change because I believe that you started your businesses to make money, enough money to have the financial freedom to make decisions that benefit you, your family and your wider community. So, if this chapter gives you the heebie-jeebies, head back to the mindset chapters and get to the bottom of your money blocks, or decide now to pull on those big-person pants and make some positive pricing changes!

Your prices should be as unique as you are, or at the very least, if they are the same as someone else, be chosen for all the right, logical reasons: reasons that suit your business and your definition of success.

From now on, when you think about your prices, remember:

1. **You and your business have a unique history and journey.** The challenges and opportunities you've been exposed to, plus your experience, mean you can't compare yourself and your business to anyone else's.

2. **What it costs your competitor to run their business is none of your business!** Those costs could and should influence their prices but have nothing to do with you and your business.

3. **You don't know what success means to your competitor**. Or what they want to achieve in this season of their business and life journey; again, this should influence their pricing decisions, not yours! You need to focus on you and what you want!

The 4 rules of pricing

1. **Define:** Understand your definition of success and what that means to you, your business and your family in this season of life. If you still need to do it, go back to chapter two and decide what success looks like for you right now and over this next period in business. This step is key before you go any further.

2. **Focus**: On your progress and forget the comparisons! You do you! What will you achieve in the next 3, 6 or 12 months?

3. **Act:** You can change your prices whenever you want to; the frequency and amount are up to you. Prices might need to change because of external economic factors like an increase in the cost of doing business, a full or empty calendar, a change of personal circumstances or just because it's been six months since you last looked at your prices and it's time for a review.

4. **Communicate**: When you share changes to your pricing structure, communicate clearly about the date it takes effect and factors that influenced the change. Never apologise for increasing your prices. And there's a full stop right there for a reason.

Okay, let's go; it's time to create profitable pricing for your business!

The Profitable Pricing Formula

As I mentioned at the start of this chapter, my Profitable Pricing Formula is something I've developed over many years in business. It's not rocket science and no doubt there are many businesses already implementing what I'm about to share – I just decided to give it a catchy name.

In a nutshell, I designed the Profitable Pricing Formula to provide you with the strategies and know-how to develop a pricing strategy that aligns with your business goals, one that captures the actual value of what you offer and pays you well to deliver it; think wages, super, profit and peace of mind.

And remember before you went into business? That time when you worked for someone else and got annual leave or sick leave, and there was someone to cover the work while you were away? I designed my formula so you can build in holidays and downtime, too.

Step 1: Let's work out your ideal working hours.

By now, you should know what success means to you in this next season of life and business, what you want to achieve, a revenue goal and what you'd like to pay yourself (your wages).

But have you thought about how many hours you want to work each day? How many days you want to work each week? And how many weeks you want to work each year? Annual and sick leave are no longer those perks you got when you worked for someone else; now, we're building them into your business, too.

If you still need to do it, gather your thoughts and make some decisions. You can always change this later and often. Brainstorming starts now! Here's a few prompts to get you started ...

What does success mean to you right now and for this next season?

What would you like your salary or take-home pay to be this year?

How many weeks do you want to work each year? Think about holidays and sick leave too.

How many hours do you want to work each week? Are there any parts of your lifestyle you want to work around with your hours, like school hours, weekends off etc.?

Now that you've got that down on paper, the next thing to think about, perhaps one of the most important, is **billable hours** because your revenue is all about how many billable hours you and your team can work in your business. We will use billable hours when we calculate your ideal working hours.

So, when you think about how many hours you'd like to work each week, realistically, how many of those hours are billable? Those are the hours when you're getting paid by someone else.

When you've got all that, it's time to work out your ideal working hours. Here's the calculation for your ideal working hours:

Weeks per year x billable hours

In my business, I like to take six weeks of annual/sick/downtime leave. Total weeks of work in a year: 52 - 6 = 46.

This means I'm available to work 46 weeks in a 12-month period.

I also plan on working three days per week.

Over those days, I'll work approximately 20 hours in total.

However, my client-facing or billable hours will only total 12 hours per week. The rest of my week will be spent on non-billable aspects of the business.

Therefore, the total billable hours are:

46 weeks per year x 12 billable hours each week = 552 hours

Based on the above example, my ideal working hours each year is 552. Therefore, I'm available to bill a total of 552 hours each year.

Step 2: Factoring in the cost of doing business

What does it cost you to run your business? That's everything it takes to keep the lights on and your business rolling. Do you know?

When it comes to the cost of doing business, many business owners aren't sure exactly what it costs them or where their money goes.

As the money rolls in, the invoices get paid and little time is spent looking at expenses until something goes wrong or there isn't enough money in the bank to pay the bills. For instance: how often have you signed up for a trial subscription only to forget all about it until a charge suddenly appears on your credit card? I'm guilty of that!

Our expenses become a means to an end, those inevitable costs you need to incur to run your business. And, for most of us, when it comes to business expenses, that's where the road ends; it's an area we only pay attention to if there's a red flag.

But did you know that reducing expenses is often the easiest place to start when improving business performance, particularly when you want to increase your profits? Undoubtedly, at some point in your career, you've worked for a business tasked with cost-cutting or done a budget where you're asked to reign in the costs. So, understanding what it costs to run your business is a great place to start when you want to earn more and increase profits.

You'll also need to know that magic number to calculate the Profitable Pricing Formula.

The best way to work out your cost of doing business is to grab the most recent profit and loss statement (P&L), ideally for a full 12 months. The

P&L will give you the total of each expense category in your business, less any tax typically added on top of that expense (eg: sales tax, VAT or GST).

If you don't have a P&L handy, you'll need to total up all your business expenses, or if you've been in business for a complete tax year, you'll find a list of your costs on your most recent tax return.

The cost of doing business includes direct costs or costs of goods sold, like ingredients to create a product or deliver your service; those non-negotiable items you need to provide to fulfil your offer.

For example: An interior designer offering a complete procurement service would sell furniture, and the wholesale cost of the furniture would form part of the direct business costs. Direct costs can also include staff costs and, in some cases, freight.

You'll also include operating costs or overheads to calculate the cost of doing business. These are all the other costs incurred to run your business such as rent, utilities, advertising, accounting fees, subscriptions, wages, superannuation and taxes, to name just a few.

The cost of doing business therefore is the total of those direct costs (cost of goods sold) plus the operating costs. It's that simple.

Your cost of doing business number is essential when it comes to pricing, so keep it handy for the Profitable Pricing Formula calculation.

MONEY MAGNET TIP:

Understanding and regularly reviewing what it costs you to run your business can help you run a lean business and increase your profit. Who wants to be paying for things you don't need, doubling up on costs, or paying for that trial subscription you've forgotten about?

Consider using this part of the Profitable Pricing Formula exercise to review your costs. Highlight areas where expenses seem high and do a deep dive. In most cases, the direct costs, those costs that directly go into delivering your product or service, can only be cut out partially, but there's always room for negotiation or improvement. On the other hand, operating costs often include obsolete, outdated, forgotten or 'nice to have' expenses.

Ask yourself what's vital to running the business, what's nice to have and what you can swap out for a free or lower-cost version. Identify areas where you might be doubling up; for example, you might pay for Asana and Monday.com but only need one. Look for expenses that are now obsolete; for example, you were paying for a social media scheduling tool but now use Meta or in-app to schedule your posts.

It's all about profit!

Revenue is for vanity; profit is for sanity!

It's a well-known saying and one that I love because, for too long, we've all been sucked into the unrealistic expectations flaunted by online influencers who assure us it's 'easy' to create a six or seven-figure business.

But as someone who has seen behind the curtain on several of those businesses, let me tell you it's not all sunshine and roses. I've worked with business owners making millions of dollars in turnover but running at a fraction of a percent in profit.

So, it's important to remember that just because the storefront of that magical multi-million dollar biz might look good on social media, there's a good chance the owners are taking home next to nothing in profit, and that's not good for the sustainability of their business, let alone their mental health.

For me, no matter how big or small your business, it's all about profit because when you're able to run your business, pay yourself, save for a rainy day AND make a profit, too, then that is where the true magic lies.

MONEY MAGNET TIP:

A profitable business also looks attractive to investors and buyers, so if you take nothing else away from this book, remember that one of the best ways to become a business money magnet™ is by running a profitable business.

And just a refresher on what business profit means – it's the amount that's left after you've paid all of your business expenses, including your wages and super; the unencumbered money or extra dollars that aren't earmarked for anything in particular, but can be used to help grow your business, add to your savings or give you a salary bump or a bonus.

When I talk about profit, I'm always asked what a good business profit looks like; what's the perfect percentage? But in reality, there's no such thing. The answer depends on a lot of different factors, for example, the stage of business you're at, whether you're in a growth phase or not, the type of industry you work in or the style of business you run, the size of your business and what your personal circumstances are, to name a few.

However, most businesses I'd suggest you aim for a profit between 5 and 20 percent, you get to decide; you might be happy with more and some of you will be happy with less. The bottom line is that you must decide on a profit number that works for you and your business in this season. You can always change your profit target and make adjustments as you go.

Putting all the puzzle pieces together – let's calculate your profitable pricing!

Okay, so by now, you should know:

1. What success means to you right now and for this next season.

2. The salary or take-home pay you want to earn this year.

3. Your ideal hours for the year ahead.

4. What it costs you to run your business.

5. Your profit number.

Now, it's time to drop it all into the Profitable Pricing Formula calculator.

If you're a fan of spreadsheets, you can find an online version of the calculator here: https://www.justinemclean.com/book-resources

Make sure you make a personal copy of the calculator before entering your information.

PROFITABLE PRICING CALCULATOR	
CALCULATE THE COST OF DOING BUSINESS	
Total Cost of Doing Business (CODB) - all expenses including Cost of Goods Sold, overheads, staff wages and superannuation, taxes	$0.00
Your Ideal Gross Wage (if not already included in the CODB)	$0.00
Plus your superannuation* (set at 11% and will auto fill in the template spreadsheet but you can calculate this manually by working out the percentage of superannuation relevant to your country - FORMULA = your salary x super percentage divided by 100)	$0.00
TOTAL COST OF DOING BUSINESS	$0.00
COST OF DOING BUSINESS FORMULA:	
Cost Of Doing Business + Gross Wages + (Gross wages X 11% or your superannuation percentage) = Total Cost of Doing Business	
CALCULATE YOUR BILLABLE HOURS	
How many billable hours will you work each week? For example: You might work a 30-hour week but only 20 of those are billable. Therefore use 20 in this calculation.	0
How many weeks each year will you work?	0
TOTAL - YOUR IDEAL HOURS	0
BILLABLE HOURS FORMULA	
Billable hours X working weeks per year = Ideal Hours	
IT'S ALL ABOUT PROFIT	
What's your profit number? Add a percentage!	0.00%
VOILA! YOUR IDEAL HOURLY RATE!	$0.00

*Calculated for Australian businesses

Here's the ideal hourly rate formula in one line.

IDEAL HOURLY RATE FORMULA:

Cost of Doing Business ÷ Total Ideal Hours X by the profit number = Ideal Hourly Rate

Here's an example already filled in:

PROFITABLE PRICING CALCULATOR	
CALCULATE THE COST OF DOING BUSINESS	
Total Cost of Doing Business (CODB) - all expenses including Cost of Goods Sold, overheads, staff wages and superannuation, taxes	$25,000.00
Your Ideal Gross Wage (if not already included in the CODB)	$80,000.00
Plus your superannuation* (set at 11% and will auto fill in the template spreadsheet but you can calculate this manually by working out the percentage of superannuation relevant to your country - FORMULA = your salary x super percentage divided by 100)	$8,800.00
TOTAL COST OF DOING BUSINESS	$113,800.00
COST OF DOING BUSINESS FORMULA:	
$25,000 + $80,000 + ($80,000 X 11% or your superannuation percentage) = Total Cost of Doing Business	
CALCULATE YOUR BILLABLE HOURS	
How many billable hours will you work each week? For example: You might work a 30-hour week but only 20 of those are billable. Therefore use 20 in this calculation.	12
How many weeks each year will you work?	46
TOTAL - YOUR IDEAL HOURS	552
BILLABLE HOURS FORMULA	
12 X 46 = 552	
IT'S ALL ABOUT PROFIT	
What's your profit number? Add a percentage!	25.00%
VOILA! YOUR IDEAL HOURLY RATE!	$257.70

*Calculated for Australian businesses

EXAMPLE OF IDEAL HOURLY RATE FORMULA IN ACTION:

(113,800 ÷ 552) X 1.25 or 25% = $ 257.70

Please remember that your ideal hourly rate is the jumping-off point for all your pricing decisions, but not necessarily your new hourly rate.

In a nutshell, it's the amount your business needs to earn for every billable hour you work. If you earn this amount during your billable working time, you've covered the cost of doing business, your wages and built-in profit, too.

This means that if you work more billable hours, for example, you won't need to earn as much per hour, but if you work less billable hours, your ideal hourly rate will increase.

If you have multiple staff or services, you will consider this when calculating your billable hours.

Example:

Zandy Consulting offers virtual coaching services, group programs and online courses. They've set their billable hours for the year at 552, and their ideal hourly rate is $257.70. They have two staff working part-time. Zandy Consulting offers services that range in price from $27 to $2,500.

They'll be working a collective of 46 weeks per year and, during each week, have estimated they can deliver 12 billable hours (552 hours annually).

In a typical week, Zandy will provide and sell various services in their business. But keeping their ideal hourly rate in mind, they know if they earn $3092.40 each week in revenue, they will meet their annual targets [$257.70 (hourly rate) x 12 billable hours].

Some weeks, Zandy will earn more than their target amount and some weeks, they will earn less, but as long as their weekly average minimum in revenue is $3092.40, Zandy knows they will reach their annual targets.

A word on hourly rates

There's no suggestion here that your ideal hourly rate should become your actual hourly rate because chances are you're not just trading time for money. However, your ideal hour can indicate what's happening within your business and highlight areas that need adjusting.

For example:

If your ideal hourly rate is not sustainable for your industry, in other words it's too high, you might need to review your pricing and create a suite of products so that you have a variety of ways people can work with you.

If you're a course creator or sell memberships or automated products, you'll need to sell enough products or memberships spots each year to cover the cost of doing business. In this case your ideal hourly rate can be used to determine how much you need to sell during a launch period or throughout the year.

You might also need to increase your billable hours, reduce your expenses, take a lower salary or decrease your profit number expectations.

If your ideal hourly rate is high, it might be worth reviewing your expenses because running your business may cost too much.

If your ideal hourly rate is low, it's time to increase your profit number or salary. You could also consider working less.

MONEY MAGNET TIP:

You'll often hear people speak about value vs worth in business, especially when it comes to pricing, but I want you to stop thinking about your prices in terms of worth. I believe that your worth is what someone else decides they are happy to pay you and that has *nothing* to do with you or the products or services you provide.

Rather, start thinking about what you offer in terms of the value you bring:

- The transformation or change you can create in someone's life with your business.

- The problem you solve.

- The time you save your clients.

- The money you save your clients.

- The experience you have and the expertise you bring to the table.

- Your IP!

- The unique perspective you bring.

- The network and support you offer.

- The impact you make!

When you consider all that value, you're probably worth way more than your clients can afford, so keep that in mind when you do your pricing.

And if that doesn't convince you to price with value in mind, consider this. My program Business Money Magnet^{TM} is an investment in time and money. In one of our recent group coaching sessions we were doing a deep dive into pricing and the concept of value vs worth.

One of my students then shared how she believed Business Money Magnet^{TM} was worth every cent she'd paid for it and that there was no real price to put on the value. The reason – she'd completed the cash flow module and implemented some of the cost-cutting measures, things she would never have considered looking at.

Through that one exercise, she not only managed to pay for the full cost of Business Money Magnet^{TM}, but she also saved enough money to take her family on a holiday too.

Chapter 13

Profitable Pricing – The Nuts & Bolts

The million-dollar question and one I always get asked is …

When should I increase my prices?

There's a better question to ask than this one, though.

And that question is: *how often should I review my prices?*

It's not a matter of finding the perfect time or moment to increase your prices. It's a matter of having a system and a structure that supports you increasing your prices on a regular basis.

Therefore, the answer to that question is simple: as often as needed.

Now that you know the jumping-off point for all your pricing calculations, it's as good a time as any to conduct a wholesale pricing review and ensure your current prices hit the mark.

Once you've completed your initial pricing review and adjusted your prices as needed, commit to reviewing your prices regularly. While there's no specific best practice for pricing reviews, here are some reasons to consider reviewing your prices:

- Your circumstances have changed – you can work more or need to work less.

- It's been a while (at least 6-12 months) since you last reviewed them.

- You need help remembering the last time you reviewed your prices.

- The cost of doing business changes.

- It would help if you had a cash flow boost and the market can support an increase.

- You've got a product or service that needs to be fixed.

- There are changes in your industry, or the market supports higher prices.

- You've improved or developed your services or skillset or been in the game for a while.

- Your competitors are charging more for the same service.

- You're booked out all the time, OR you've got lots of white space in your calendar.

- Your expertise has increased and you can justify a higher price point.

Of course, when we talk about increasing prices, it's important to note that increasing your prices can initially impact your customer base and sales. Consider testing new prices on new clients only and offering a pricing structure with a smaller increase to current or loyal customers, or a transitional period of three to six months as they adjust to the new pricing structure.

You can always use discounts and promotions to welcome new customers into your business or offer your existing customers a one-time discount before prices increase.

MONEY MAGNET TIP:

Increasing prices is a fact of life, but remember, it's your business, so you can choose how and when you increase your prices. Whether it's a wholesale increase or an increase on a single item, an increase for new clients or all of them, it's up to you.

The bottom line is that to maintain profitability, you'll need to regularly review and adjust your prices, so don't be afraid to make changes when necessary.

Sharing the news of a price increase

When it comes to price increases, one of the sticking points for many business owners is when or whether to share the news. Sometimes, the thought of telling people about your new prices is enough to stop you from moving forward, but here are my thoughts when it comes to sharing the news.

Decide if you need to share or not. Sure, you'll need to tell your existing customers, but your new customers don't need to know. When they come into your world, your price is the price; it's not the 'new' price. Of course, the exception here might be a referral customer, but all you need to say is that prices have increased. Simple!

When you're increasing prices for existing clients, give advance notice. It doesn't need to be much notice, a few weeks will do. If you get pushback from existing customers, rather than keep them on old rates, suggest offering them the old rate and delivering 80% of the same service for their existing rate, for example.

Another option is to prepare a list of the services you currently provide for your client, outlining the most important tasks, those that are essential to get the job done to the tasks that you believe can be paused for now.

You then can renegotiate a new price for the reduced suite of tasks. Often your client will be shocked at what you're doing for them and while they might opt for the shorter to-do list now, when the money is flush again, may opt back into the additional services.

Be honest with your customers. You don't need to make up elaborate stories, apologise or give long-winded explanations about your prices. Choose one reason for the price increase, for example, an increase in the cost of doing business and keep your explanation simple.

Sweeten the deal with added value – What added value can you offer that won't blow out the cost of the service but make it look more attractive? Add something to the service that's cost-neutral to you – for example, a Canva template or social media calendar template.

Remember, not everyone will be happy with your price increases, and that's okay.

Here's an email template to help you share the news:

Subject: *Important Update Regarding Our Services*

Hi [Customer Name],

How are you? I hope this email finds you well. I wanted to share some news regarding our services.

The cost of providing high-quality services has gone up in recent months. To continue offering the level of service that you've come to expect from us, we're increasing our prices by [percentage or amount].

The new prices will take effect on [date]. We understand that this may be a difficult change. But we are confident that our services will continue to offer exceptional value for the price.

If you have any questions or concerns, please don't hesitate to reach out. We value your business and look forward to continuing to serve you.

Best regards,

[Your Name]

MONEY MAGNET TIP:

It's important to remember that the tone of your communication is just as important as the content. Use a professional, friendly, and understanding tone to help ease the transition for your customers.

The do's and don'ts when it comes to pricing

DO:

- Increase your prices when needed, but give your existing customers a heads-up.

- Explain the reason for the increase, but never apologise!

- Look for ways to reduce the cost of doing business in lockstep with pricing changes.

- Consider taking a smaller profit.

- Ponder the prospect of increasing the billable hours you work.

- Add to your service offerings or diversify your services so your ideal clients can work with you at varying price points.

- If needed, reduce the number of services and focus only on the most profitable ones.

- Change your money mindset around increasing prices.

- Review prices regularly!

DON'T:

- Reduce your wages arbitrarily or stop paying yourself.

- Stop setting aside savings for tax.

- Stop paying yourself superannuation.

- Forget about the profit altogether.

- Work yourself to burnout.

- Undervalue yourself and stick with your old pricing structure.

- Neglect your customers or sacrifice the quality you offer.

- Ignore market conditions.

When your price increase doesn't go according to plan

If you feel bad about increasing your prices, you keep apologising for the increase or immediately want to discount your services, I want you to consider: perhaps it's you, not them?! Maybe it's time to change your money story, focus on your value and remind yourself why you started in business. Remember, you're running a business, not a charity!

Your first step is to think about how you can deliver your services more efficiently.

Ask your team or peers for ideas about streamlining or automating your services to save time and money. Now is the time to think outside the box and not give up!

Alternatively, it might be time to get real; is it worth continuing with the service if the numbers simply aren't there?

Just because you've always done something doesn't mean you need to continue to do it. Remember, it's your business, your choice. Do you need to add a different service, one that makes more money or changes the ratio of services you offer?

Food for thought

No doubt increasing your prices can get tricky, so if you're coming up with reasons *not* to increase your prices, even though you know you need to, consider these:

- **You don't need to increase your prices across the board.** Pick one service and only increase the cost of that service.

- **Grandfather prices for your regular or most valued clients.** Only new clients must pay the new prices.

- **Know your business and industry and where the tolerance levels for a price increase exist.** Sometimes, you might need to work within those parameters, so if that's the case, consider adding different, more profitable services to your ascension model.

- **Look for growth opportunities in your existing business.** Consider adding new income streams to diversify your revenue; reach out to like-minded business owners and suggest a collaboration or service swap to increase visibility or save on expenses; create packages rather than offering a stand-alone service.

- **Is it time to add a surcharge?** If your clients want a quick turnaround on one of your services or expect you to work around the clock to meet a deadline, consider adding a surcharge for expedited service.

- **Be careful with the quotes.** Build an expiration date on any quotes you send out so you can be sure you're still making the money you need to cover your costs. There's nothing worse than someone coming back six or twelve months after you've sent out a quote and expecting a service for an old price.

- **When times are tough, review your costs and prices often.**

Pricing Psychology

There's always a lot of chatter about the psychology of pricing and using its various techniques to get your prospective clients over that sales line.

While pricing psychology is a whole other book, it's worth mentioning here because there's been a lot of study around the science behind consumer behaviour and pricing decisions. It's certainly something to consider when setting your prices. By understanding how customers perceive prices and using this knowledge when you set your prices, you can master the art of pricing to drive sales, maximise profitability, and impact your business's success.

But when it comes to pricing psychology, there's lots to consider, factors like perception, emotions, cognitive biases, and social influences that, in turn, influence customer behaviour, create perceived value, and optimise your business's financial performance. So, here are some pricing psychology principles you might want to consider:

Anchoring

Anchoring is a powerful pricing technique that involves presenting a higher-priced option to make other options seem more affordable.

Example: Offering a premium package at $199 next to a standard package at $99 can make the latter seem like a steal. A real estate agent may start the bidding process for a house at a high price but then lower it to make it seem like a better deal. Or an electronics retailer may advertise a laptop for $900 and mention that similar laptops from competitors are priced at $1,200.

Decoy pricing

A concept similar to anchoring, where a less attractive option is offered to make the item you want to sell appear more appealing. This technique is about subtly nudging your customers towards your preferred offering, the thing you want to sell more of or like to do most in your business.

Example: A restaurant may offer three menu options – a $15 small salad, an $18 'big' salad, and a $20 salad with grilled chicken. The $20 salad with grilled chicken is the desired option, the $18 'big' salad serves as a decoy to make the $20 option appear more appealing.

Framing

Similar to both anchoring and decoy pricing.

Example: a clothing store may advertise a dress for $200 but then high-light that it's made from high-quality materials and was previously priced at $400, making the $200 seem like a bargain.

Charm pricing

Using charm numbers like 7 or 9 and ending prices with those odd numbers, $97 or $199, has a psychological impact on customers. Research suggests that people perceive prices ending in odd numbers as lower than they actually are, so there's a little bit of magic in those numbers. By utilising this strategy, you can create a perception of affordability while maintaining your desired profit margins.

Example: A toy retailer sells a product for $19.99 instead of $20. This technique exploits the psychological phenomenon that people perceive prices ending in .99 as significantly lower than prices ending in a whole number.

Get rid of the cents

This one applies particularly to the service industry because taking away the cents on a price, whether that's in your proposal or on your website, can make a number look smaller and, therefore, make it seem like it's a cheaper option.

Example: A copywriter sends out a quote for website copy but instead of quoting $2,000.00 simply quotes $2,000.

Price bundling or packages

Price bundling or offering 'good, better, best' packages is a strategy where you offer multiple products or services as a package deal at three different entry points. It's also known as the power of three!

It's all about bundling up a group of services and then offering them as a package for what is perceived as a discounted price. It appeals to customers because it suggests there is value-for-money and they're getting a great deal.

By offering a selection of three similar, but different package options, the 'good, better, best', the customer feels like they have more control over their buying decision.

Research suggests that in most cases customers will go for the middle option, because the 'good' option is seen as the cheapskate option, the 'best' option is seen as an indulgence or more expensive option, but the 'better' option is seen as excellent value for money. So, the lesson here is to make the 'better' option the thing you like to offer or want to do the most in your business.

Example: A social media manager offers Silver, Gold and Platinum package services. The Silver Package offers to create and schedule 4 posts per month using existing templates. The Gold Package offers to create and schedule 6 posts using bespoke templates, captions and hashtags. The Platinum Package offers everything in the Gold Package but also includes an additional 4 posts and a monthly client strategy meeting.

Limited-time offers

Scarcity is a powerful motivator, and limited-time offers to tap into this psychological trigger. Creating a sense of urgency, such as 'Only 24 hours left!' or 'Limited stock available,' can push customers to make quicker purchasing decisions. These time-limited offers create a fear of missing out and drive increased sales during the promotion period.

Example: A car dealership may offer a limited-time promotion for a $1,000 discount on a specific model to encourage customers to purchase before the promotion ends. A business coach may do a limited-time launch with a cart open for only one week encouraging prospective customers to buy before it's too late.

Social proof and price perception

I'll have what she's having! Humans are social creatures, and we often seek validation from others before making decisions. Influencers anyone! So, incorporating social proof into your pricing strategy, like using influencers, can significantly impact your business.

But it doesn't need to be as costly as using a high-profile influencer; instead, displaying positive customer reviews or testimonials on your website and social media can influence others to work with you or buy from you. Highlighting the experiences and satisfaction of past customers can help establish trust and enhance the perceived value of your products or services.

Example: A T-shirt designer sends a range of shirts to a micro-influencer and in return asks for a post on Instagram promoting the t-shirts. The micro influencer receives free goods and the business and the business a marketing plug to a new audience.

Why pricing psychology matters for your business

Implementing pricing psychology techniques can benefit your business in multiple ways, and by taking the time to understand your customers' psychological responses to pricing, you can:

- Boost sales and revenue by strategically influencing customer behaviour.

- Create a perception of value, allowing you to charge higher prices for your services.

- Stand out from your competitors by adopting innovative and persuasive pricing strategies.

- Build customer trust and loyalty by aligning your prices with your ideal customer's preferences.

Now that you've unlocked the secrets of pricing psychology, what strategies will you implement in your small business?

The Mosman Mentality (no offence to anyone living in Mosman)

Back in the late 90s, Mosman, a leafy suburb north of Sydney, was the sought-after place to live for the up-and-coming set; back then, we used to call them Yuppies. I lived much further north, had just had my second child, and on this day headed to the local mall to get the kids out of the house.

We were having morning tea, a decaf for me and baby Cino and brownie for my eldest, and an older lady asked if she could join us. Of course, I said yes, seats were scarce, and it would be nice to have an adult conversation.

Naturally, we were talking kids; she also had two sons, albeit much older, so we had something in common. As it turned out, one of her sons was a prominent obstetrician in Mosman. His mum, clearly very proud of her son and his achievements, talked about his large family and the incredible work he was doing in the medical field. Mentioning that it was just as well he was so successful because he had a lot of kids to look after and they were expensive. But, she also mentioned that he'd recently had a life-threatening medical episode and had been told that he needed to halve his workload, stat!

'But doc, I can't do that,' he's reported as saying, 'I've got kids to feed, clothe and educate!' It was about then that his doctor told him to make the change or risk further, much more severe consequences. According to his mum, this sent a shock through her son; he knew he needed to find a solution to his dilemma quickly.

So as legend has it, he went into his surgery the next day, immediately doubled his prices and told his staff they needed to take half as many new clients. Seemed like a great solution!

Word quickly spread in Mosman and surrounding suburbs about the local OB charging over-the-top prices for his services. But rather than having the expected impact, a decrease in new enquiries, what happened next shocked everyone. The practice was inundated with women who wanted to see the 'famous' OB; the perception that he was twice the price of every other OB, so he must be twice as good.

And if you believe his mum, before long he was booked solidly again, this time making double the money!

Now, I've never gotten to the bottom of how true this story is or how much of it was embellished by a very proud mum. But I hope the Doc survived, thrived, lived a long and healthy life, helped all his patients and made lots of money in the process.

After all these years, I still remember the story clearly. At the time, we had very little money and I thought it was all a bit crazy, but I'd also shared it with a friend who lived in Mosman and she wasn't surprised. I recall her saying 'Oh, that's the Mosman Mentality. The more expensive it is, the better.'

In hindsight, I now realise that the 'Mosman Mentality' is true in many situations we find ourselves in when deciding to purchase something. Honestly, how many times have you thought it's more expensive? It must be better. And that's the power of pricing psychology!

So, next time you're setting your prices and worried they're too high, think of this story before you choose to decrease them. Inevitably, you'll find your ideal clients who choose you **because you're the most expensive**!

Pricing stories – you might see yourself here ...

Aerin's story

Aerin owned a small creative business, a solo operation, which suited her just fine. Aerin had complete control over who she worked with, the type of work she said yes to and how often she worked. Aerin was so popular in those early days of business that she was spoiled for choice.

The problem

However, there was a big problem with scope creep in Aerin's business; clients signed on to get tasks A and B completed but then, as the job continued, added tasks C through H! Not one to upset her clients, Aerin always agreed to the extra tasks. Sure, she'd charge additional fees for the work. But, because these were unexpected additions to the original job, invariably, these extra tasks overlapped with the next job and caused a lot of unnecessary stress.

When Aerin started working with me, she was still working on a job scheduled for completion six months earlier. The job was ongoing because Aerin had allowed her clients (let's call them the Joneses) to add additional task upon task, scope creep at its best! Not only did all these additional tasks eat into the time allocated for her new clients, but the Joneses were still on 'mates-rates', a rate Aerin had gladly offered two years earlier as a favour to a friend. Just to add to the workload, they were Aerin's most demanding clients.

Now, two years in business is a long time, and in that time, not only had Aerin's costs increased exponentially, but her business was struggling under the weight of those extra costs. Time was scarce, and Aerin spent any extra time in her day working for the Joneses, taking their calls or answering their emails. New leads had stopped completely, the outlook looked gloomy, and Aerin had stopped paying herself a regular wage.

After completing the *Profitable Pricing Formula* process, we discovered that Aerin was severely undercharging the Joneses and all her clients. So, we put in place a new pricing structure for any new clients coming into Aerin's world and a slight increase in pricing for her existing clients.

The solution

Aerin chose to add her new prices to her website and then communicated the price increases to her existing clients. The email was well-written, easy to understand and made perfect sense. Aerin even built a time buffer before the increase would kick in, allowing her existing clients to wrap up their jobs, if needed, beforehand.

All of Aerin's existing clients wrote back emails communicating their confidence in Aerin and their willingness to pay the new rates; one even suggested that Aerin increase her rates immediately.

All but one. You guessed it. The Joneses.

The pushback

Sadly, the Joneses took great offence to the new rates. Remember, they were still on mates' rates, so the increase to their rates was still far from what her other clients were paying. They threatened terrible reviews and said they'd refuse to pay the new rates and any of Aerin's outstanding bills if she went ahead with the increase! Within 24 hours, they sent word that they'd decided to terminate Aerin's services and intended to find someone else, someone 'more reasonably priced'.

Naturally, Aerin was inconsolable. While she wasn't too worried about losing the Joneses as clients, she was concerned about the bad reviews and the thousands of dollars in unpaid bills. So, what did Aerin do next?

The outcome

Aerin decided to continue working for the Joneses at the original 'mates-rates', hoping the job would 'wrap up soon'. Not a great ending to the story, right?

The final fix

I'll be honest – Aerin's decision made me a little crazy. Unsure why she would tolerate such poor behaviour from her clients, and unwilling to leave things as they were, I needed to get to the bottom of why Aerin had made her decision. After some long, soul-searching chats, here's how we problem-solved and eventually got Aerin, and her business, back on track. If you're in the same boat now or find yourself in similar territory somewhere down the track, this may help you, too.

1. First, we did a deep-dive into Aerin's money story – her attitudes and beliefs regarding money, self-worth and money values. As we uncovered her thoughts and beliefs, we questioned each one, asked if they were true and why, and then wrote a new money story that was positive and looked forward with abundance rather than scarcity.

2. We decided on a review of Aerin's ideal client and created the perfect client avatar for Aerin's future business. Essentially, it was all about choosing the type of person Aerin would enjoy working with, one who shared common values and would not only appreciate the work Aerin provided but would be happy to pay for it, too.

3. Then, the business comms got an upgrade, so every word spoke directly to the new client profile. From the website to social media, the lead magnet and freebies to the weekly newsletter, it all focused on helping Aerin's ideal client solve their number one problem.

4. We also put in place a visibility campaign to get Aerin out and about and in front of her ideal client as much as possible and increase her profile.

5. We took another look at Aerin's pricing to allow her to employ a freelance virtual assistant. We decided to hold the current pricing for two months and then do another review and increase prices for new clients.

6. We created straightforward job outlines, expectations and dead-lines for every new job, and put deposits and progress payments in place for all work. With an upfront 'contract', the idea was that clients would know what to expect and when and clearly understand from the outset what any additional tasks would cost them.

7. Finally, we drew up an exit plan so that Aerin could wrap up her work for the Joneses in a win-win way. It wasn't as easy as it sounds, but in the end, we got there; Aerin got paid for her work and even got a well-earned, positive Google review.

Today

I'm thrilled to report that clients are knocking down the door to work with Aerin and now at industry-premium rates. Aerin no longer puts up with scope creep, has a kick-arse team and spends her time on money-making tasks like selling. Aerin's net profit has improved, and she's finally paying herself a good wage.

Victoria's story

Like many of my clients, Victoria has a business offering administration services, including social media support, calendar management, travel bookings, presentation preparation and some writing services. The business employs four full-time staff and has continually made a 20 percent profit year-on-year.

Victoria is one of the few people I work with who religiously reviews her prices every six months with no prompting from me. I love witnessing the confidence she has around pricing, too.

The problem

When Victoria started her business, she was one of the first VAs on the scene, so from the outset, her services were in demand, allowing Victoria to scale and grow her business without too many issues.

However, in late 2023, as the economic climate in Australia and the USA became more challenging to navigate and with costs increasing in all business areas, more and more small businesses needed help to make ends meet. Victoria noticed that her long-standing clients, those whom she had happily worked with for many years with no issues, began to complain about her prices and question every service Victoria and the team completed. 'Did it really take two hours to schedule a month's worth of social media?' complained one. 'Surely, you can complete a blog post in less than an hour, so why is the charge so high?' said another.

Every day, it seemed a new email arrived, or another phone call came in complaining about pricing. Some clients sent emails deciding not to continue their working arrangement with Victoria and business were looking dire for the first time since she began her business.

The solution

When we jumped on Zoom for our regular monthly mentoring session in early January 2024, Victoria was in tears. She'd just had another call from a long-term client questioning a bill and wanting to terminate Victoria's services. It was clear we needed to do something, stat!

So, here's what we did next:

1. We completed a wholesale review of the business's pricing, explicitly focusing on the expenses. After identifying several thousands of dollars in cost reductions, we also reviewed staffing and the current demand for work and reallocated the existing workload so that all staff were working to capacity. We then determined new prices for each service.

2. Next, we looked at each client who had recently complained about invoices, wanted to 'break up' with Victoria, or had already left the business. In each case, we made a comprehensive list of every service Victoria and her team provided, noting roughly how long the service took to deliver.

3. Victoria, along with her team, undertook a process review to determine if there was a more efficient and cost-effective way to deliver services in the business.

4. Together we then drafted bespoke emails to each client, explaining that we acknowledged their budget constraints and the season of business they were in. In each case, we outlined the services Victoria and her team currently undertook for that client and ranked them from most essential service to least important or nice-to-do but non-essential service.

5. In the email, Victoria suggested a new working arrangement that would allow her clients to get the help they needed but also enable them to save on their service costs. They could maintain their long-standing relationship with Victoria, complete the essential tasks, and save time and money.

The outcome

While the process took a great deal of time, effort and communication, there's no question that it benefited the business. In every case, even where clients had already left the practice, this exercise allowed Victoria to retain and/or reengage 100 percent of her clients.

In addition, Victoria uncovered a pattern of the most sought-after services her business offered and then added this to her value ladder of services as a new profitable service.

In so many cases, when clients leave or push back on price, the natural reaction is to be annoyed, upset or make yourself feel bad; it must be something you're doing wrong. But, by simply putting yourself into your client's shoes and taking a moment to empathise with where they are in business, it's possible to see a solution that will keep everyone happy.

MONEY MAGNET TIP:

No matter who you are or what type of business you run, someone will always have a problem with your prices, and that's okay!

The key to your success starts when you understand that when it comes to pricing, the only people who matter are the ones who see you, the value your product or service offers and who will pay the price that you've decided on; the price that you know will allow you to run a profitable business, where you get to pay yourself a wage, save for your taxes and your future and have money to stash away for a rainy day!

Chapter 14

10 Simple Ways to Embrace Good Business Money Habits

'We are what we repeatedly do. Excellence, then, is not an act but a habit.'

Aristotle, via Will Durant

For most business owners, managing the business money can be an overwhelming task, especially if the finance side of the business isn't your thing. When you've already got too much on the to-do list, and that space between what you know and what you think you need to know can seem too big to navigate.

And while that could be the best excuse ever to leave the business money for 'later' or hand it over to someone else, it's only a short-term solution.

Whether you're just starting in business or have been in the game for a while, and no matter how good your financial know-how is, improving your finances and becoming a business money magnet^{TM} is easier than you think – and it all comes down to 10 simple habits!

Plus, once you get going, it can all be done in as little as a few hours a week, an hour tops if you're running a small business – I promise.

Over many years in business, the game-changer for me and my clients has been introducing smart money habits into day-to-day business life. The right money habits can help increase your cash flow, protect your assets, secure a bright financial future for yourself and your business, and help you achieve your success dream.

In this chapter, I'm sharing the tried and tested money habits I've collected over the last 30 years in business. These habits will help you eliminate the feeling of being overwhelmed and, most importantly, save you time and money.

But, before you dive in, a word of warning. As you read through these good money habits, you'll be inspired. You may then be tempted to try and adopt them all, or most of them, all at once. And while I'd encourage you to incorporate them all into your business over time, I'd also encourage you to habit stack; start by incorporating one new habit, get it bedded down over a few weeks, and then add the next one. Cherry-pick the habits you're not currently embracing and add these to your business first. If there are habits you already include, why not review them to see if they need a boost? Alternatively, look at all the habits and choose what will help you and your business move forward immediately with confidence.

Remember, good habits start when you make time to incorporate a single thing into your business or life. From there, it's all about consistency. When you've got one habit going well, add another one to the mix and repeat. Habit stacking is one of the fastest ways to improve your business and life, so get stacking as soon as possible.

1. Incorporate Money Monday or Finance Friday

Consistency is critical, which is why this habit will improve your life – especially if you've never had time to look at the numbers.

Incorporate a Money Monday, Finance Friday or whatever day of the week works for you (I couldn't think of a compelling enough alliteration for the other days!).

Set aside an hour on the same day every week, add it to your calendar as a recurring meeting and here's the most important part: make it non-negotiable.

Once you decide to do it, it's as simple as turning off all distractions, showing up and sitting in the discomfort of the business money for one hour a week. Treat that hour with yourself and the money just like you'd treat an appointment with a paying client. In other words: only cancel in case of emergency!

Once you're working in your money hour, you can do things like:

- batching all the finance tasks

- reviewing the numbers and profit and loss statements

- checking cash flow and invoicing

- chasing late payers

- paying bills or setting up direct debits.

It may sound like a lot, but you can achieve it all when you batch the business money in only a few hours each week.

Initially, the task list might be overwhelming, so start with a small set of tasks and add to it as you go. Eventually, you'll have a comprehensive list of tasks to complete each week that are bespoke to your business.

Here's what my Finance Friday looks like:

1. Open Xero and reconcile any outstanding transactions.

2. Check on payments received and follow up with outstanding payers.

3. Create new invoices and send them to clients, or update progress invoices and send them out.

4. Check the bank account to make sure it all looks in order.

5. Pay any outstanding bills by their due date. If bills have arrived through the week but aren't due for a while, I schedule them as a future payment so it's a 'one-touch' system. In other words, I'm handling things only once.

6. Check on or make transfers for tax savings and profit and ensure no hiccups.

7. Review and update the cash flow forecast to ensure the funds needed over the months ahead are in the bank or about to arrive.

8. Open the Profit and Loss Statement, look at the numbers and ask these questions:

   a) Did I get the income I expected?
   b) Do the expenses appear in order?
   c) Is my net profit number on target?

If you use a bookkeeper or other finance professional in your team and they're managing the money for you, then your allocated finance time each week is the perfect opportunity to check in with them and get a picture of where the business is at and what next steps you need to take.

Plus, when you're in the finance head space, you're more likely to consider more significant, strategic decisions based on the numbers.

2. Review your spending

As entrepreneurs, we're often distracted by the new, bright, shiny objects presented to us almost daily. Buying things that save you time or grabbing that email copy template because it's only $27 is tempting! We've all been there. But in my experience, all those insignificant expenses can quickly add up to a large chunk of your business revenue. Subscriptions are some of the biggest culprits here.

Matthew, a client and Aussie business owner, has been in business for years. His number one goal is to make his business successful. However, Matthew and his business were in a world of pain, with cash flow in crisis, increasing amounts of debt and stress. And the worst part, he didn't know why.

What you need to know about Matthew though, is that he loved those US-based marketing gurus who were always selling the latest course or products. Things that would help accelerate business and make easy money. So, he was always tempted to buy their latest offering. In many cases, the monthly subscription was less than $100, so trying it out was a no-brainer.

The only problem was that Matthew always forgot to cancel those trial subscriptions or memberships or the ones that he tried but quickly realised didn't work.

When I arrived on the scene and did a deep dive into why the business was running at a loss, I started with the expenses. I soon uncovered over USD$3,500 in unused monthly subscription or membership costs. No wonder the business never had any money!

As I know first-hand, it's an easy trap to fall into. And depending on the supplier, getting out of your subscription can be more challenging than it should be.

Some subscription-offering businesses will lock you into an annual sub-scription, even if you pay monthly, so there'll be a hard cancellation date sometime in the future with no cancellation or money back until you've served your dues. Others will make it almost impossible to cancel, so my advice here is always to read the fine print, and if the price seems too good to be true, then there's probably a catch somewhere that will have you paying for way longer than you imagined.

The bottom line is to do a regular, monthly, at best, or at least quarterly review of all business expenses.

As you work through this process, ask yourself:

- Do you still need this service, system, or thing in your business? Should you downgrade to a free version or cancel altogether?

- Are you doubling up on a business tool? If so, choose one and hit cancel on the other.

- Are you still getting value from the items you're paying for?

- Can you get a better deal on utilities, energy, phone contracts, subscriptions and incidentals?

- Each month, could you target one area of your business, for example, your phone plan, and call the supplier and ask for a better deal? You'll be surprised at your savings at the end of an entire year.

- Are there more innovative ways to get help and save money? For example, a contra-deal with a supplier.

- Is it time to ask your regular suppliers to do better deals and give you discounts or extended terms?

There's no doubt that you'll save money by regularly reviewing your expenses. So, every time you do a review, I challenge you to find one obsolete expense and hit the cancel button.

3. Keep an eye on ALL the numbers, not just the dollars in the bank

There are many numbers to monitor in your business, and not all relate to money.

Some of the best performance indicators have little to do with the dollars in the bank. However, the health of these KPIs will impact your business bottom line or net profit.

So, when it comes to the business numbers, you need to broaden your horizons. Consider all the numbers that can impact your business and decide which key numbers you need to keep an eye on. The best time to do this can be during your dedicated business money time each week.

I'd recommend building in an extra hour once a month to monitor some of your key business numbers. Create a simple spreadsheet to keep track of your numbers and update it according to your overall business plan. Here are some key numbers you might like to focus on:

- **Cash in the bank**: This one relates directly to the money side of the business. However, this number is a great day-to-day indicator of what's happening in your business. Once you get into the swing of your regular weekly money hour, you'll have a pretty good idea of what your operating bank account should look like, it will almost become second nature. Using your online banking app to log in to see how the dollars are tracking makes this quick and easy.

  But this only works if you're using a single bank account for all of your operating ins and outs, so a final word on bank accounts: keep your business bank accounts for business only, and if you're tempted to dip in for a personal payment or you need a salary bump, be sure to either repay the money to your business account or take a look at your personal budget so your weekly wage covers everything you need to pay.

- **Sales/orders:** As part of your goal setting, you'll no doubt have come up with the number of sales, orders or new customers you want to see in your business each week or month. Tracking this number each month, or more often if you need to, is a good way of staying on target.

- **The cost of doing business:** After you've done a deep into your expenses and know what it costs to run your business each year, you can monitor monthly to ensure you're staying on track.

- **Customer retention rate:** This number tells you how many existing customers choose to keep working with you and how often they take advantage of your services. For most business owners, continuously acquiring new customers is costly, so work out how to continue working with the customers you already have. What will keep them coming back for more? Your retention rate will depend on your industry, but aim for a minimum of 35 percent.

- **Customer enquiries:** No matter how good your customer retention rate is, a mix of 'old' and new customers is the key to business sustainability. According to the Rule of 7, a marketing term bandied about since 1903, the average new client will need to see your advertising materials or encounter you seven times before they commit to buying. Keeping tabs on the number of new leads and your customer conversion rate can help you determine whether your messaging and sales pitch are working. If you get lots of inquiries but your conversion rate is low, there might be something wrong with your sales pitch; are you asking for the sale at the end of the call and then following up with your prospective client?

If your lead generation is low, consider different ways to get customers into your business ecosystem.

- **Social media numbers:** If you use social media as part of an awareness or new business strategy, keep tabs on your monthly social numbers. Keeping tabs on the number of followers and engagement will help you determine what's landing with your ideal client and what's missing the mark. But remember, you don't just want vast numbers of followers; engagement is way more important because these people are more interested in what you're sharing and selling.

- **Mailing list numbers:** If I had a dollar for everyone I worked with who either didn't have a mailing list or had one but didn't nurture that list, I'd be a rich woman! So many business owners rely on social media's power to sell. They believe a huge social media following is directly linked to business success. But I'm calling BS on that!

Don't get me wrong, social media is a necessary evil in business. It helps with visibility and credibility and is the 'social proof' people seek to see if your business is legit. There's no question it's a powerful tool because, done well, it's that first exposure to you, your business and what you're all about. However, social media is rented space and as we've seen so often over the last few years, when you don't own that space, the landlord can take it away from you at any time.

So, keep tabs on your mailing list numbers!

Remember, your mailing ties back directly to customer enquiries and new leads and is essential for two reasons; number one, if someone has taken the time to sign up for your newsletter or download your thing, they immediately go from being a cold client to a warm client, someone who is likely to convert. Unless they unsubscribe, you won't have to worry about them finding you on their daily scroll again.

The second, arguably more important consideration, is that your mailing list is a business asset you own and that no one can take away or turn off. It can also make your business more attractive to a potential buyer or another brand eager to collaborate. But it's also an asset for your day-to-day business because it's an immediate pipeline to your warm clients. It's an information platform where you can share your values and expertise and offer services.

So, I'd encourage you to start or grow your mailing list. And when you've got those warm leads in your world, love them hard.

Now, if you want to get a little more advanced, other numbers I recommend you keep an eye on are:

- **ROI or Return on Investment:** This is a way to measure the impact that marketing and advertising can have on your business's bottom line. A positive ROI in the range of 5-7 percent is seen as a reasonable expectation.

  Example: if you've paid for a series of Facebook ads, look at the number of leads generated and calculate the cost per lead. Facebook will share this information but if you want to calculate it yourself, it's simply – cost of the Facebook (advertising/marketing) campaign divided by the number of leads.

You can then determine if that cost per lead or return on investment is worth it and decide if you should continue this type of advertising or look for a more cost-effective way to spend your advertising dollars.

- **Cost per acquisition:** Significant if you spend money on advertising; this is the cost of acquiring a new customer. A positive CPA will depend on the type of business you're running but most businesses will convert at between 2 and 3 percent.

  Example: your Facebook ads have generated 100 new leads but not all of these leads will convert to paying customers. So, your cost per acquisition is what it costs you to convert a client. To calculate this you use the formula – cost of the Facebook (advertising/marketing) campaign divided by the number of customer conversions (customers who have purchased).

- **Order Value:** A great one for retailers or anyone in the product-based industry; this is the average value or dollars spent each time a customer orders.

  Example: your retail business has 100 orders each day. Order value varies from $20 to $99. To calculate the average order value use the formula – Total of all the orders for the day divided by the number of clients, in this case 100. The result is the average dollar value of each sale or what you can typically expect each customer to spend in any one purchase.

- **Lifetime Value:** Is the revenue you make from a customer over their lifetime of buying from you or working with you, essentially predicting how much money you can expect from an average client if you manage to retain their business over a long period.

Example: a business coach converts a client to their low-cost $27 offer but then also manages to convince that client to sign up for their group coaching program at a cost of $1,997 per year. The customer has been in the business ecosystem for a full 12 months and so in this case, the lifetime value of the customer is $2,024. If the customer is retained, the lifetime value will increase as they buy more services.

You can also measure website traffic, churn rate, bounce rates, employee turnover, revenue per employee, training spend, revenue vs budget forecast, inventory turnover and customer satisfaction.

While there is a long list of numbers you can choose to measure in your business, I'd keep the list to around ten key numbers that tie directly into your business goals for this next period of business. Like everything else in business, what you choose to measure and how often can change, so stay open minded to the areas of business that you need to stay on top of to achieve your goals.

As you complete this exercise, the last thing you want to do is become overwhelmed, so once you've set up your spreadsheet and the KPIs (key performance indicators) you wish to measure, consider outsourcing the task each month. But whatever you choose to do, be consistent and make a date to measure and analyse all your business numbers often.

4. Spend your time making money

Is it time to call in the experts?

There's no question that no one will understand your business as well as you do!

And when you're just starting out and funds are tight, you dive in and do everything needed to keep the business running. That often means countless hours googling 'how-to' or watching YouTube videos on the areas of business you could be better at to save some money. Let's face it, in the early days, the last thing you'd consider is outsourcing or paying for help.

However, whether you've been in business for five minutes, five years or longer, a helping hand can make all the difference. Finding an expert to do the jobs you aren't good at or don't like can save time and money and leave you more time to do more of the things you're great at doing.

A good habit to adopt no matter where you are on your business journey is to ask for help when needed. Yep, when you have a problem, or there's an area of your business that's a time suck, don't second guess the money, call in the experts!

Here are some reasons to get some help:

- You've learnt all you can about a particular area of business but still don't get it.

- It takes longer than needed to complete a task and a specialist can do it in half the time.

- You don't have the time to monitor particular areas of your business consistently.

- You're in a bit of a mess, and you need help to clean it up.

- It would help if you had guidance when it comes to business strategy.

Make sure whoever you choose is the right fit for your business. Their job is to help and guide you, not condescend, make you feel stupid, or show off. If hiring an expert is in your future, before you hire someone new here are my tips:

- Ask around for recommendations – word of mouth is often the best way to find the best people.

- Book a free discovery or strategy call and ask how the expert can help your business grow. Have they done it for themselves or do they have a track record of helping others achieve a particular goal that's not on your list?

- If you're using a professional contractor, make sure they are registered and have all the necessary insurance.

- Ask for testimonials.

- Choose someone who you gel with, who shares your values and can work with you in a way that will help you achieve a particular outcome. For example: if you know you need some tough love, choose a person who is prepared to keep you accountable!

While there will be an initial outlay in time and money, the idea of outsourcing is that in the long run, it will help you get back time and make more money!

So, even if you've got all the tech and systems and processes in place, if you're constantly being pulled in ten different directions, maybe it's time to make a list of all of the things you do in your business and decide what you can delegate to an expert, what you need to do yourself and what you can safely dump.

You've heard it before, and I will repeat it: to make more money and not burn out, you need to work smarter, not harder.

5. Save for a rainy day

We've all experienced the whirlwind that's been the last several years in business. One thing I know for sure is that the clients who had rainy-day savings and a plan to future-proof their business have managed to get to the other side almost unscathed.

But the reality is that saving money, especially when funds are already tight, is easier said than done.

When I first started a business savings account, as I mentioned, I was in debt with the tax office to the tune of $42,000. I knew I wanted to create a savings nest egg but had no clue how to manage it. All the research I was doing around business money back then kept coming back to the same thing – aim to set aside three months' worth of trading expenses, including wages, as soon as possible.

At that time, my first thought was that I had more chance of winning lotto or flying into space than achieving that target. But despite my reluctance I gave it a go. It took me nearly three years to save those three months' expenses!

I started very, very small. My savings amounted to coins and the occasional five-dollar bill going into a money box. But once I'd made a start, opened an online savings account and began to see the balance grow, I became addicted to increasing that balance, even if it was only by a few dollars every week.

The best way to start or accelerate your savings plan is to first open a dedicated savings account. Then set up a cash flow forecast for your business. That way, you know where the financial peaks and troughs are occurring – where you need to save for business expenses and where you have extra that can go to your rainy day savings account. Your cash flow forecast can also help you work out a weekly amount you can afford to transfer and forget without putting yourself or the business under financial stress.

No matter where you are in the money and business journey, I guarantee that you'll never regret making a commitment to save. It's all about making a start and then being consistent because it all starts with intention and following through!

> **MONEY MAGNET TIP:**
>
> U Once you decide on your savings target, make it fun, and give your account a name or a goal.
>
> If the worst happens and your savings take a hit now and again, don't dwell on it; just start over!

6. Protect yourself: Does your insurance stack up?

I have a love-hate relationship with insurance. It's one of those expenses I'd rather not have to have, but something I'd never do without because I can't predict the future.

It's important to me to protect myself, my business and my family because as life often shows us, it usually costs a lot of money when something goes wrong.

And because I'm no insurance expert, every year since the beginning of my first business back in 1994, I have spoken to my insurance broker, Val, and arranged for her to sort out my insurance.

Val is a gem because she comes back to me with a comprehensive report that shows me the coverage I need, what's changed over the last year and what it will cost me to get covered. I typically get three recommendations. The service is free to you because it's likely that the insurance agent gets a commission from the insurance company, but it's a service offered by many insurance brokers out there, so shop around, ask about commissions involved and always choose an agent you like.

While I get to make the final decision about my insurance, using a broker gives me peace of mind that an expert has guided me and I have up-to-date insurance that meets all the legislative requirements of running my business.

So, make sure your insurances stack up! This annual habit is one I recommend you adopt immediately.

> **MONEY MAGNET TIP:**
>
> You don't have to consult an insurance brokerage expert, but I'd highly recommend it.

7. Set a financial goal and make it achievable!

As I've mentioned, business goal setting should always include a financial goal because it gives you a solid focus for the future and can help set you up for success. But, finance goals can be daunting and if you've ever tried to write your business-money goal and found yourself staring at a blank page, you're not alone.

Trying to set financial goals for business can often lead you back to your money blocks or comparing yourself with other business owners setting (and achieving) outrageous money goals! So, if you can relate or find setting a financial goal for the year ahead difficult and are unsure what your goal should be, simplify the process and start by looking at what happened in your business last year.

- What did you earn?

- What did you pay yourself?

- What was your net profit?

These numbers and how the business performed can give you a jumping-off point for your next goal.

You can then create a goal based on the back of what's already happened, and instead of shooting in the dark, start with a goal to improve these numbers by a few percent on the previous year, for example.

There's no right or wrong regarding financial goals, but regardless of what everyone else is doing, start by keeping your goals simple and realistic. SMART goals if you will. A SMART goal is Specific, Measurable, Attainable, Realistic and Timely.

I love a lofty goal as much as the next person, but if you're new to goal setting and want to make it a habit that sticks, then not overcomplicating your goal and making it realistic will make you more likely to achieve it and do it all over again.

Plus, when you start by setting a realistic financial goal for your business, your overall strategy becomes more manageable, too. You'll be more likely to set that stretch goal once you get close to your starting goal. And if you feel the overwhelm creeping in, break your goal(s) down into smaller, manageable steps, and before you know it, you'll be ticking them off the list.

8. Invest in yourself and your business

There are no shortcuts to business success, but one of the best ways to get from where you are now to where you want to go in the fastest time possible is to ask someone who has been there, done that to help you and invest in education.

Whether that's education via a course, development via a network or one-to-one assistance, investing in yourself, your staff and your business can help your business grow and succeed.

This one's a habit for the start of the year, each new cycle in your business or when you identify the weak spots in your business – when you want to improve, look for someone to help you get there fast.

MONEY MAGNET TIP:

On my regular Facebook scroll, I often come across posts asking for business coach or business course recommendations. The replies are always in the hundreds and I venture to doubt that the poster is more confused about what the right next step is than when they made the decision to post.

So, whether it's a business mentor, coach, strategist or a business course, here's some money magnet tips to keep in mind:

First, decide what specific area of business you need help with. While there are lots of coaches out there, just because you used to work in marketing, for example, doesn't automatically make you good at business. So, choose the sort of coach you need. If you need help with marketing, choose a marketing coach; help with sales, choose someone with sales experience; help with the business finances, choose a qualified business money expert.

If you need all round business help or strategy, at the very least, choose a mentor who has run a successful business in a similar area to your business and who can back that up with proof. You wouldn't choose that person with an interest in cars to fix a problem with your car, you'd go to a qualified mechanic, so be just as discerning with a business coach.

So many coaches, course creators and mentors don't understand what it's like to walk in your shoes. It's not about choosing someone who is two or three steps or years ahead of you either; a good business coach is someone who has a wealth of varied experience and who has had to work through all types of business problems and find solutions.

You don't need to sign up for long-term mentoring or coaching packages or get locked into a mastermind, ever, so choose wisely and understand the fine print and the get out clause.

Every coach you work with will be good for a season and once that season is done it might be time to move on. There's no point working with someone out of loyalty or because you were locked into a great rate and if you leave now, it will cost you more to come back. The bottom line, if you're no longer learning or getting something from your coach it's time to move on and that should be ok!

Buy courses that have clear outcomes and that will ultimately help you learn something new and save you time and money.

And finally, while we're on the subject of investing your way to success, this could also include investing in better systems and processes, better tech or equipment or additional staff.

9. Get Good at invoicing

You do the work, you invoice, and get paid, right?

Not always.

You have to get good at chasing up invoices to keep your cash flow ticking over. This habit seems like a no-brainer. When you improve your invoicing process and make it a regular part of your weekly task list, you will improve your cash flow.

It's a simple and painless task, plus there's a reward at the end: money in the bank.

Unfortunately, for many business owners, it's not that easy. The reasons range from no time to a deeper, more concerning issue around fear – what will the client think, will they challenge my invoice, what if they don't pay me? And so, this relatively straightforward task gets pushed off to do some time in the future, and it's true of service and product-based businesses and wholesalers, too.

That would be okay if it wasn't for this little thing called cash flow, which happens to be vital to the success of every business. So, it's time to get good at invoicing!

Here are my suggestions to make invoicing as pain-free as possible.

1. **Set aside time every single week to review and send invoices:** Make it part of your Money Monday or Finance Friday routine. Send invoices for completed jobs or progress payments for on-going jobs, update invoices for work completed over the last week, and follow up outstanding invoices with an email or a call.

2. **Make it easy for your clients to pay you:** That means an invoice that's easy to understand and includes all of the details that your client needs and none of the details they don't!

3. **Forget handwritten or Word Doc invoices, use cloud ac-counting to send invoices:** Cloud accounting systems allow you to create invoice templates and have time-saving features to send invoices and follow up with overdue payers.

4. **Offer a variety of ways for your clients to pay you:** Direct debit is the most cost-effective method for your business. But it might not suit your clients, so consider using third-party payment services like Stripe, Paypal, or even Afterpay. Each has pros and cons, including costs, but if they help make life easier for your client and you get paid faster, it's a win-win!

5. **Add your up-to-date bank details to your invoice if you use direct debit:** I know that one seems like overkill, but I've worked with business owners who forgot to add bank details to their invoice and wonder why they aren't getting paid.

6. **Shorten your payment terms to seven days:** Your cash flow will thank you for it!

7. **Overdue invoice? Don't wait to chase bad payers:** For me, even one day overdue means it's time to follow up. Set up automated reminders in your cloud accounting system to go out once the invoice due date has passed. And if you're concerned that chasing up an outstanding invoice might impact your relationship with your client, create a fictional accounts team with a dedicated email and send follow-ups from that email account. The bottom line is that money is better in your pocket, so step up and follow up!

8. **Product-based businesses:** You wouldn't expect to go into a store, take a whole lot of stock and tell the store owner you'll pay them later, right? Keep your wholesale customers from doing this to you! Always get deposits or full payment on any wholesale orders placed, and before the stock leaves your warehouse, make sure you've been paid in full.

9. **Service-based businesses:** Take non-refundable deposits for longer-term project work or work that requires the purchase of materials. Are you offering one-to-one coaching services, a keynote or another one-and-done service? Then, consider asking for an upfront payment for the service. There's nothing worse than chasing someone for money after the fact for something you've delivered.

And, if you're delivering a longer term service, send out regular progress payment invoices. There's little point waiting until the end of a long-term project to get paid. That might work for your client, but during that time, you need to think about how you'll keep your business running without the cash flow.

A note on bad payers ...

At some point in your business life, you'll meet a lousy payer or a complaining customer who insists on a refund.

In the case of the bad payer, the best advice I can offer is to talk to your client. In most cases, bad payers won't respond to emails, whether from you or your fictional accounts team, but in nearly all cases I've encountered, they will respond to a phone call. Ask what the problem is and how you can help them solve it. Believe me, in this scenario, you'll catch more flies with honey, so be nice; it's just a conversation between grown-ups.

However, not everyone feels comfortable talking about money, especially when it comes to chasing up a late payer, so if you're concerned about making a call, I'd suggest asking your bookkeeper, if you have one, to make the call on your behalf.

Regarding refunds, the best practice is to have iron-clad T's and C's and ask your customer to acknowledge these before you start working together, then stick to them! But here's the thing with refunds. While we all hate giving a refund, sometimes, even if your client is well outside the Ts and Cs, a refund is the best way to move on from a difficult client or situation.

A few years back, I worked with a demanding client. I won't go into all the details here; suffice to say, we had a six-month contract, and during each of our hour-long sessions, my client would always have 'just one more question' right after we'd hit the finish time. The question was always urgent, and couldn't wait until the next session, so the people-pleaser in me always took the time and answered the question. Pretty soon, I was well behind on my six-month contract, so it was costing me to work with this client!

As we arrived at the end of our six months together, the client still had a single session to use. But despite numerous emails from me following up to book something, there was radio silence. After several months of chasing, I gave up.

Eventually, 13 months after our contract was up, the client emailed me, insisting they wanted to use up their last hour. But they also had a laundry list of what they wanted to achieve during that time; impossible in just one hour. While I was happy to honour that last hour of coaching and could have charged additional fees to spend more time with the client, my business had moved on. I had moved on and was no longer doing that type of work. So, I processed a refund for the last hour of coaching. While I thought I'd be annoyed as I hit send on the refund, I felt great relief and empowerment and knew I'd made the right decision.

MONEY MAGNET TIP:

Collecting money should be the easy part of business, but sometimes, it can be one of the hardest things to do. By putting in place some simple, tried and true practices and getting in the habit of getting good at invoicing, it soon becomes one of the most accessible areas of your business to manage. When that inevitable bad payer or annoying customer comes along, you can deal with it knowing you have the cash flow and the best practices in place to keep your business going strong.

---

10. Pay yourself NOW!

When we work for someone else, we're used to our salary arriving in the bank on 'pay day', no questions asked. Likewise, we quickly get into the habit of making that money last until the next payday, so the cycle continues.

However, when we start a business, we start at nothing, no income, quite a few expenses, some savings or a buffer so we can live while we build, but rarely on the list of those expenses is our wages. One of the most common questions I get asked by business owners is, 'When should I start paying myself?'. And my answer is always the same ... NOW!

There are a few reasons for my logic.

The first is to start as you mean to continue: create a business built from the get-go to cover the cost of doing business, your wages, superannuation and a profit.

The second, paying yourself, even if it's not your usual corporate salary, is a mindset hack. It reinforces the value you bring to the business and yourself and that you're 'worth' the investment, aka, wages. Naturally, when you are starting out, those wages may not match your former corporate salary, and you'll be thinking you're 'worth' a lot more, but you get the picture.

Of course, the realist, numbers gal in me also knows that paying yourself when you start a business is easier than it sounds, particularly when you have no paying clients. So, before you take the plunge into business, it's ideal if you can set aside at least three months of corporate salary so you can keep going on the home front while the business is established. Let's call it the 'wages nest egg'.

Then, decide what you want your business salary to be as you kick things off. If you're making nothing, there'll be nothing to draw as a salary, and you'll need to rely totally on your wages nest egg, but the idea is to pick a number here. Depending on the business you run, you might be happy to take a few hundred dollars a week in wages, or you might like to take more of a profit-first approach and take 50 percent of every dollar you earn as wages. The decision is yours.

But, whatever you choose to take in those early days, always allocate money from your wages nest egg to top up and keep the personal budget balanced and a stable wage coming in each week. Just like when you worked for someone else, deposit your salary into your personal account once each week and then make money last until the next payday. Only be tempted to dip into the business operating account to take extra wages if it's an absolute emergency.

Now, if you're already well established in business, and the wages nest egg is long forgotten, but you're still not paying yourself a wage, here's what you need to do next:

1. Review the cost of doing business and get your number.

2. Decide on your salary for this next season.

3. Head back to the pricing chapter and work out your profitable pricing ideal hourly rate. Then, with these numbers and your profit number in mind, do a wholesale pricing review of your offers. Look at your services; what must you change, add, or delete to attract your ideal client? One who can pay enough to cover all the business costs, your wages, superannuation and savings.

Now, if the numbers still aren't cutting it or you can't afford to pay yourself the wage you'd like to in this next period, it's time to take a realistic look at your personal budget. What does it cost you to live, and where can you make some savings to give your business the best chance of success?

In other words, what's the minimum salary you need to make it all work without working outside your business to top up your wages? When you know, go back to the pricing drawing board, use the minimum viable salary and take another look at how the numbers stack up.

Whatever you do, pay yourself something and start today. The bottom line is if you're not making money from your business, you've got a very time-consuming and expensive hobby, and none of us goes into business as a hobby!

Put it into practice:

Your 10-point action plan to get started with good business money habits:

1. Decide on a regular weekly date and time to focus on the business money – start with an hour.

2. Now that you've got the date and time, block it out in your calendar.

3. Create a to-do list of what you want to achieve in your money hour.

4. Decide on the numbers you want to track; that's all the numbers, and set up a Google Doc or spreadsheet ahead of time to help you keep track of those numbers.

5. Know where to find the reports and information you need for maximum money-hour efficiency.

6. Make a note of the due date and amount of each of your bills, especially those subscriptions and add them to your calendar for the money-hour the week before they're due so they're top of mind. You can take action to find some savings.

7. Set up direct debits for your wages, superannuation and regular payments.

8. Set up a direct debit for your rainy-day payments.

9. Create your financial goals for the next twelve months.

10. Decide where your time is best spent and what expertise your business needs. If you last spoke to your accountant or finance professional a while ago, start there.

Checklist: Great habits to take into a new financial year

The end of the financial year can be overwhelming for small business owners, especially when you're the one doing everything. So, here are my tips and sure-fire habits to make a fresh start in the new financial year or whenever you're ready to move on from overwhelm.

☐ Implement cloud accounting software in your business, and if you already use it, ensure you're taking advantage of everything it can do for your business.

☐ Put solid systems in place to deal with the financial side of your business:

- Deal with receipts or bills the minute you get them.

- Create a folder or folders in Google Drive or use your online accounting software to keep track of your financial documents.

- Batch your tasks, think Money Monday or Finance Friday, spend a solid hour and finish the work.

- Automate where you can.

☐ Have one business bank account, your operating account, for all the ins and outs.

☐ If finance isn't your thing, or you don't like dealing with that side of the business, call in the experts sooner rather than later. Remember, it's a tax deduction.

☐ Know what you can and cannot claim from the get-go! Get professional help, even if it's just at the start, so you get it right and maximise your tax return.

☐ Create an asset register and add to it every time you purchase a new capital.

☐ Talk to your accountant about a financial plan for your business.

☐ Know what compliance obligations apply to you and note critical dates.

☐ And while we're talking compliance, create a plan and commit to saving for that and a rainy day.

☐ Create a budget and a cash flow forecast.

Chapter 15

Unlock Your Earning Potential and Become a Business Money Magnet

'The more you learn, the more you earn.'

Warren Buffet

Ever wish you had a key to unlock a magical door that led you on the path to making more money? Or the ability to think about your business idea and manifest the success (and money) you wanted?

Ah, if only it were that easy!

Whether you've been in business for a short time, a long time, or are still in the planning stages, you soon realise that the path to success is not a linear journey but a road filled with lumps and bumps, triumphs and challenges. And even when you think you've finally reached your destination, there's bound to be a curveball that will set you back, or a new goal or idea to aim for that will propel you onto an alternate route and the new highway ahead.

While the business journey can be precarious at times, it can be equally rewarding and over my 30-year career as a business owner, I've been lucky enough to learn some tricks and strategies to help you become a business money magnet™ and unlock your earning potential, no matter where you are in your business journey. Spoiler alert – they're not all money focused but, in my opinion, all roads lead back to the business money.

So, let's dive in.

Who are you working for – what's your niche?

Throughout the book, I've touched on the importance of getting educated, improving your financial literacy, and understanding all those business money basics. We've also touched on why choosing your unique definition of success in this season of life and business is vital and how to set and achieve financial goals in your business. All of these things are stepping stones on your journey to unlock your earning potential.

When you choose to start a business, you've likely got an idea or transformation you want to sell as a product or service. Sure, you'll have some idea of who would benefit most from what you're selling, but ultimately, as the business kicks off, you hope people will find you and buy your stuff.

But, no matter who you are, what you're selling or how well you've set up your business, even if you've targeted those people you can best serve, when weeks go by and there's no one knocking at the door, panic can set in. Before you know it, instead of sticking to your marketing plan and selling to your ideal customer, you're happy to sell to anyone and everyone, ideal client or not!

I've definitely been there, but with the benefit of hindsight what I know to be true, is the sooner you name and claim your ideal client, and focus on them exclusively, the better.

When you decide who you're speaking to, your ideal client, you get to actively chase after work with more of the people you love, those who appreciate what you do and are happy to pay you for your work and expertise. While it's tempting to take the money from wherever you can get it, especially early on in business, you'll get to a point in your journey where working with anyone is no longer fun because, truth bomb, only some are your ideal customers. And the 'anyones' will eventually end up being more trouble than they're worth!

That's where the idea of niching in business comes in: essentially finding that specialised or focused area of the broader market where your products or services can do the most good and be in high demand with your ideal clients.

Have you ever been told to find your niche?

Here's the thing about niching: in my opinion, it's redundant, because no matter what sort of business you have, **you** are your niche. So, if you're still looking for your niche, please stop!

What do I mean by this? Well, even if you're working in a saturated or specialised area of the market, what you bring to the table and how *you* offer a particular service or suite of products is likely to be different from anyone else in your industry because you're you, and you're unique.

For example, I'm a Business Money Mentor, but only a short time ago, I had a whole income stream in my business where I offered day-to-day bookkeeping and compliance services. Now, bookkeeping and dealing with compliance have been around since people invented business. In all honesty, it's a pretty straightforward service offering and almost the same no matter where in the world you're working.

But where my business was different to the business down the road was in the unique qualities and feel I brought to the services my business offered; from the way it looked on the outside, to the way the services were delivered.

From the outside, my branding and messaging were different compared to most others in the same industry. I chose shades of pink to represent my business, when everyone else had either blue or green branding and I spoke to my audience in simple terms instead of using 'accounting speak'.

Internally, my clients would often describe me and the way I delivered my services as a 'nice warm hug' for their business finances. Essentially, what my clients meant was that unlike all the other compliance businesses out there, I delivered my services without judgement and in a way that those *'I don't do numbers'* clients could easily understand. In other words, typically me!

For my business, it meant and still means that creative business owners seek me out for my services and financial education because they know I get them. They're happy to work with someone who understands.

Now, I didn't set out or niche into working with creative businesses, but these are largely the clients I attract. I'm creative at heart, so I understand their business, but more importantly, I know how I'd want someone to explain the finances to me, and that's what I offer my clients. As it turns out, they love me and I love them back.

I also get to work with lots of other business types too, but in ninety-nine percent of cases, the business owners who find me are the ones that need my special brand of support.

All of this is to say that while you don't necessarily need to decide on your business niche, you should determine your business values, how you want to operate and lean in to what makes you and your business unique.

Working out your ideal client

Once you've got your niche sorted or made the decision to lean into your uniqueness, it's all about identifying your ideal client, that someone you'd be happy to work with every day of every week.

Finding your ideal client really is one of the keys to a happy and successful business, because as you uncover and understand your ideal client, you'll also know how to speak to them, and more importantly, sell to them. And in a business age where customers want to buy from people with shared values, people they like, understanding who you're speaking to means you'll be able to better explain what you do and how you can help.

So let's work out your dream client!

Close your eyes for a minute and imagine that your ideal customer has found your website, product or service. You can see exactly who they are – what they look like, their gender and age.

Miraculously, you also know how they think, what they like and dislike. You can hear their voice and experience all of their emotions; it's almost like, for a moment in time, you've become your ideal client.

Now, describe that customer: the single visitor to your site or store.

Write down everything you can remember about them, including their name. The aim is to get to know

that single customer so well that you could easily step in their shoes. When you start by understanding a single customer, you'll realise who you're trying to serve and why.

You'll also understand their problems and how you can help solve them with your products or services. Better still, you'll know how to create the messaging that will encourage them to go from a brand lurker to a buyer, or even better, a loyal brand ambassador because if your ideal customer is happy, you'll get repeat business, lots of referrals, and you'll be satisfied too!

Dig deep, dream away and write down everything you can remember about your ideal customer. Use these questions to help.

Remember, you're talking about one single customer here.

1. What's the name of your customer?

2. How old is your customer?

3. What does your customer look like? Write down as much detail as possible.

4. Is your customer single or in a relationship, do they have kids or ageing parents? What does their household look like?

5. Where does your customer live – country and city? Are they renting, do they own a house, or have a mortgage?

6. Does your customer work, and what's their average annual income? Is money tight, or do they have money to spend?

7. Is your customer the primary decision-maker when buying your products or services?

8. Now, think about your customer's beliefs, their goals and values – what's important to your client?

9. What annoys your customer? What don't they like?

10. What are their hobbies, or what do they do in their spare time?

Do they read books and magazines? Are they sporty or creative? What TV shows or movies do they like?

11. Does your ideal customer attend events or go to conferences? Do they follow any teachers, authors or industry experts? If so, who?

12. Do they have any guilty pleasures, and in their heart-of-hearts, what's their biggest dream?

13. What are their favourite brands?

14. Do they hang out on social media? If so, what platform?

15. How can you help your customer? What pain point can you help them solve or what's a transformation you can help make in their lives?

16. How does your customer want to feel when engaging with a favourite brand? Happy, energised, inspired?

17. What lead magnet or free offer might encourage your ideal customer to share their email address or reach out for a free strategy call? Think of the words and pictures that might motivate them.

18. And finally, what would make your ideal customer say WOW about your brand and keep returning for more?

All this information will help you form a complete picture of your ideal client. This way, you can tailor your messaging, products, and services to meet their needs.

You might be tempted to come up with more than one ideal client while doing this exercise, but I encourage you to find that single ideal customer first before you consider any secondary clients.

Remember, your ideal client is the person you want to work with the most, the person on the top of your yes list who is happy to do the work, pay your price and be your biggest fan.

MONEY MAGNET TIP:

Your ideal client is likely to evolve as you and your business change and grow, and that's okay, so review your perfect client at least once each year.

Business is a numbers game

The bigger your audience, the bigger the potential to sell more of your thing/s.

And the more you sell, the more money you earn!

So, it's little wonder that in this digital age, where the best marketing platform you have sits in the hand or the handbag of your prospective clients (yep, talking about the smartphone here), business owners are fixated on social media, increasing audience numbers, engagement and hopefully sales in the process. For many business owners, it's the only marketing tool they use and all of their marketing efforts, plus a good chunk of their time and money, is spent creating new content for social media platforms.

But, as someone who started their business when social media wasn't around, while I understand entirely the fixation, relying on social media to boost my business is a fool's errand. It's like building a business on a rented space, and honestly, like playing a game you can't win!

And that's just how the moguls who own the platforms like it!

You could call my son Lachy an influencer. When writing this book, he had a combined following of more than 2 million followers on his platforms. Recently, as we chatted about viral TikTok videos and Reels, I asked him what he believed was the one thing that sent a TikTok or Reel over the edge into viral territory, and was there a formula that worked every time?

As someone who has had a few of those viral videos (that's Lachy, not me), he made a comment that stuck with me: "social media is a little like gambling". His logic was that no matter how big or small your account, now and then, the social platform of your choice delivers you a jackpot; a post or video that goes 'viral'.

Now, viral for Lachy might be a few million views in a couple of hours; viral for me is a thousand views over a couple of days. But no matter what viral is for you, when you hit the jackpot, you feel like you've finally worked out the algorithm and uncovered something that works for your social account. Was it the hashtags you used, the shirt you wore, the length of the reel, or the caption? Even though there's no real way of knowing, in that viral moment, you're convinced that social media is the way to go, and you keep coming back for more, making more content, spending more money on ads and countless hours scrolling for ideas. Can you relate?

If I told you there was a better way to market your business that didn't involve social media at all, one that could become a long-term asset for your business and make it easier to sell, would you be interested?

Now, I'm not suggesting for a minute that you ditch social media because there's a place for socials in your business. For example, I use social platforms to show the world I'm a real person, to stay visible, magnify my voice and chat with other business owners. But I don't rely on it. Instead, my marketing weapon of choice is my email list.

> **MONEY MAGNET TIP:**
>
> Every business, no matter how big or small, should have an email list as the cornerstone of their business marketing strategy.

Easy, inexpensive, effective

When I think of my 30 years in business, most of my business has come from my email list or word of mouth. My email list is an easy, inexpensive, effective way to turn those cool-lukewarm clients into raving fans. Plus, it's been a sure-fire way to unlock my earning potential and I'm sure it will work for you, too.

If you haven't already got an email list in your business, it's time to get a wriggle on.

Starting your email list is as simple as gathering the emails of everyone you've worked with during your business life. You can also consider family and friends who might enjoy hearing what you have to say and adding them, too. After all, family and friends can be some of your best business advocates.

Next, sign up for email marketing software. There are many options on the market, some with free versions, but all with similar features and benefits. I use Flodesk because it has excellent templates, is easy to use, and I can schedule the emails to my list well in advance.

Once you've created your email list, don't make the mistake of thinking it's all about selling because no one on your list wants to be sold all the time and it's the fastest way to get people to unsubscribe.

Instead, use your email list to speak to your ideal clients, nurture them, and give them information for free, peppered with subtle selling. Of course, if you have an offer, a new product or service, use your email list to sell, but this is about community, warming up an audience who hopefully will buy from you one day.

How do you grow your email list?

According to *Optin Monster*, 60 percent of people who come across your business and have the opportunity to download a freebie or sign up for a newsletter will sign up for your email list, but only 20 percent of those same people will choose to follow you on social media. Hopefully, you've got your messaging right and that 60 percent are your ideal clients. This is a huge opportunity to unlock earning potential, and when you've got your email marketing set up and a welcome email sequence ready to go, you can then get really intentional and grow your list.

The best way to do this is with a lead magnet, a free or low-cost resource, or an offer to gather contact details, specifically emails. These days, consumers are more savvy regarding email lists and whom they share their contacts with. So, make sure whatever you choose as your lead magnet has value, a quick win or transformation.

Some lead magnet ideas include:

- checklists
- quizzes
- eBooks
- mini-courses
- cheat sheets
- coupon codes
- free shipping

- templates

- free trials.

Growing your email list can be challenging at times, but keep at it, keep growing and most importantly, keep nurturing your list by sharing value. You'll be surprised how many people on your list eventually choose to work with you.

MONEY MAGNET TIP:

An email list can also be a valuable asset if you choose to sell your business.

Prospective buyers with access to a list of potential buyers will often pay more for a business because a list can equate to opportunity and sustainability.

Network like a Ninja!

As an absolute introvert, networking was always the last thing I wanted to do!

Going to an event and making small talk, particularly when I was there solo, seemed like hard work, so I often gave networking events a wide berth. Then Covid happened, and networking went online. We used social media, Zoom and Microsoft Teams to stay connected with our friends, colleagues and business buddies. It was a more straightforward way to network, no awkward meet-cutes or trying to muscle in on a group of mates for a chat, but everyone in a virtual room connected (often while still in their PJs). It exposed me to the power of networking.

Now, post-Covid, we're spoiled for choice regarding networking opportunities, with both online and in-person events happening in tandem, making networking more accessible than ever.

But why do you need to network? And how can networking possibly unlock your earning potential?

I always say you should leverage the contacts you've got to get the connections you need, because there's a power in the brain's trust you choose to surround yourself with. These people will help you when you need it, share ideas, listen, and recommend you to people when you're not in the room, and there's power in that, too. And if you believe those sayings, that *'You're the average of the five people you spend the most time with'* [John Roth] or *'Show me your friends and I'll show you the future'* [Dan Pena], then you know it's vital to surround yourself with the best people.

Certainly, in my experience, having a network of like-minded business friends makes business life a little less lonely, but more importantly, having friends in the right places and on speed dial means that when I need help in my business, I've got people to call on. For that reason alone, networking is a gold mine.

Undoubtedly, the people in your network, those you surround yourself with, are the most influential. So, get networking like a ninja and use the power and influence of your network to help your business grow and unlock your earning potential in the process.

Curate your YES list!

Do you value your time, or does the people-pleaser in you put everyone else's needs ahead of your own?

One of the simplest and fastest ways to unlock your earning potential is to value your time. Your time is one of the most valuable resources you have to offer, so curate your YES list!

- Say YES to what you like doing; the things that light you up!

- Say YES to your A-list clients and make the rest wait!

- Say YES to the opportunities that help your business grow, in other words, make sure they're a good fit!

- Say YES to investing in yourself!

- Say YES to an increase in your prices!

- Say YES to 'me' time and treat yourself!

- Say YES to you!

MONEY MAGNET TIP:

If it's not a hell YES, then make sure it's a hard NO, because when you say yes to something, you're giving up time, energy and mental space to do it and inevitably saying no to something else.

Embrace your unique voice and elevate your digital presence

People buy from people, and there are people out there who want to buy from you. So be YOU!

Forget about trying to emulate that other person offering the same services as you; instead, embrace your unique voice and use it in every business area. From your dealings with clients to your web copy, emails and marketing, business today is about understanding who you are, what you stand for and how you can help your ideal client and then shouting that from the rooftop.

If you've been reluctant to speak up or share too much of yourself with your audience, think again.

I'm not suggesting you share every personal detail of your life or every thought that enters your head. But, the fastest way to get a loyal following is to show up as you and share your story and values with the world.

It's time to embrace your unique voice and elevate your digital presence by being you because the world needs what you have to share.

Create a digital media strategy

In today's online world, your business has the potential to reach customers everywhere, so take the time to elevate your online presence.

Spruce up your website – DIY or call in an expert here to help:

- Is your design clean and easy to read?

- Add new and engaging content.

- Share and demonstrate your expertise.

- Ramp up your Search Engine Optimisation to make it easier for your ideal client to find you on Google.

- Check website speeds, backlinks and performance.

Create your digital media strategy:

- Pick your platform(s).

- Be consistent both in tone of voice and how and when you show up.

- Share valuable information – remember it's not about you, it's about helping your customer.

- Repurpose your content so you're not creating something new for every channel.

- Create 4-5 content pillars (topics you speak about regularly) to keep your content consistent and help you create content more easily.

- Find ways to batch content and create tasks.

- Use tech to save you time on posting.

- Set a limit or choose specific times to engage with your audience.

- Consider regular live stories or Q&As.

- Don't make your digital strategy your main marketing tool, think smarter.

- Don't rely on social media, build that list!

Focus on the customers you already have

If I surveyed a room full of business owners and asked them the fastest way to increase revenue and unlock their earning potential, would they choose: A) engaging new clients or B) working on repeat with clients already in your business ecosystem?

When I've asked this exact question during workshops and talks, the most popular answer by far was option A) – engaging new clients.

Most business owners think getting new clients through the door is the fastest way to make more money. And while there are lots of pluses when a new client shows up, the key to creating a sustainable business is understanding how to retain and re-engage former or existing customers. Why? Because retaining a client or re-engaging a former client will cost you way less time and money than bringing in someone new.

There's no outlay on marketing and advertising, fewer resources are used to set up and onboard an 'old' client, and because you already know who you're working with, you're more likely to complete the work faster, too.

So, focus on the customers you already have and those customers you've worked with in the past. Anticipate what they might want next, get proactive and reach out with suggestions on how you can continue to help them.

> **MONEY MAGNET TIP:**
>
> A study out of *Bain & Company and Harvard Business School*[1] shows that an increase in customer retention by only 5 percent can lead to profit growth of between 25 percent and 95 percent over a period of time! Way to unlock some earning potential right there!

Fail fast, forward and fearlessly; learn and move on

About one in five small businesses fail!

There are lots of different reasons, primarily associated with money, but every time I hear about a business failure, I can't help but think about Thomas Edison and the invention of the light bulb. When a reporter asked him how he felt about failing 1000 times before he finally got it right, his reply at the time shocked the world. 'I didn't fail 1,000 times,' he said, 'The light bulb was an invention with 1000 steps'. If only we could all think of our failures in this way.

In 2024, we're all still a little afraid to fail. Usually it's because we don't want to be judged, and let's face it, failing isn't fun, so it's not something any of us would choose.

When David and I started our toy shops and e-commerce sites back in 2002, the one thing we always said was that it would be okay if we failed, as long as it didn't cost us a lot of money. Well, we failed more than once – with our debt with the tax office and our first (and last) foray into wholesaling – and in both cases, it cost us a lot of money, but we learned.

In my case, life was changed forever by that tax office debt. And as for wholesaling, at the time, it was a minefield of dodgy international traders, language barriers and bad luck, but the learning was invaluable and set us up to avoid repeating the same mistakes.

The reality is that to succeed in business, sometimes you need to take a risk; sometimes you'll win, and sometimes you won't. However, taking that risk can be the difference between the status quo and levelling up your business and your revenue.

So, my advice is to take calculated risks, and if you fail, fail fast, forward and fearlessly. Learn from your mistakes, try not to repeat them, and keep moving forward without fear, regardless of what anyone else might think.

Mentors can be magic

Mentors, coaches, or whatever you want to call them can be invaluable in your business – magic if you will!

If they've got a track record in business and the qualifications, there's no doubt that a good mentor or business coach can accelerate your business journey, help you unlock your earning potential and get you to where you want to go in the fastest time possible and hopefully without any missteps along the way.

However, some mentors and coaches can lure people in with outrageous promises, like 'Work with me and I'll show you how to make seven-figures in your business in a few easy steps', or who work with the belief that they don't need to be a true expert but rather just need to be a few steps ahead of the people they're helping.

No matter what industry you're in or the type of business you run, there'll always be brand new 'experts' telling you how to make it work and that they have the secret to success; all you need to do is pay to play, but in my experience, that's not true.

As a Business Money Mentor, I know the difference I can make in someone's business. But I also understand that every business case is individual. No matter how familiar the type of business is, there's always that x-factor that shows up, and my thirty years of business experience helps me navigate that x-factor and get results for my clients.

So, while I encourage you to think about working with a business mentor to help accelerate your business, here are my tips for making sure you choose the expert who's the right fit for you and your business.

Why do you need a business coach or mentor? What do you need help with and what is your end goal?

When you know, look around and find mentors or coaches who can help you with your specific needs. Then book an initial free strategy call with the mentor or coach and ask them to share what they've achieved in their business. Are these results typical of what you want to achieve?

Ask the mentor or coach to share what results they've achieved for others, what industries they have worked in, and who they've helped. Would they be happy to share testimonials?

Are these results sustainable, and what is required to achieve them over time? Ask for specific examples. For instance, is that business they helped to seven-figures a business who achieved that revenue target by spending fifty percent of their income on Facebook ads and whose company didn't make a cent in profit in the year they made those seven figures. Remember, if it sounds too good to be true, it might just be too good to be true!

Ask for recommendations from other business owners, if they'd be willing to share their results when working with the mentor or coach, and how that coach has helped them.

How do you get on with your potential mentor or coach? Can you see yourself working with them? Are your personalities in sync?

Does the expert you're engaging expect you to sign a contract? What's the fine print and the exit clause?

The right mentor or coach can make a massive difference to your business in a relatively short period. But before you go down the mentoring path, ask yourself this one final question: are you the sort of person who can work with someone who will tell you what to do, uncover and share the hard truths and push you to achieve those things you said you wanted to accomplish in that initial discovery call?

If the answer is yes, then go for it, sign up and give it a go. But remember, mentors don't always need to cost you the big bucks. If there's a business owner out there that you admire, what not reach out and see if they'd be willing to spend an hour with you and talk business?

Do it – Dump it – Delegate!

The three Ds of business and a surefire way to unlock your earning potential and become a business money magnet^{TM}!

Why? Because your time is your most precious resource, it costs money, and when you spend your time working in an area of your business where you can do the most good, you'll say goodbye to overwhelm and help your business make more money.

No one knows your business better than you do. So, rather than waste hours and days doing admin tasks or hack-work, do the work that you started your business to do. If you started your business to create advertising campaigns, for example, forget bookkeeping and social media, especially if these aren't your strengths, and outsource them to a specialist who can complete them in a fraction of the time.

Embrace the 3-Ds of business and start by writing a list of all the tasks that are needed to keep the business running.

On a sheet of paper or spreadsheet, create three columns – the DO IT column, the DELEGATE IT column and the DUMP IT column. Then, divide the business tasks into those columns.

The DO IT column will contain tasks you need to do yourself.

The DELEGATE IT column tasks you should consider delegating to an expert, team member or contractor and the DUMP IT column, those tasks that have either been on the to-do list forever or are nice-to-do but non-money generating tasks.

DO IT	DELEGATE IT	DUMP IT
Sales call	Bookkeeping	The idea of inbox zero

Once you've completed the list of tasks, think about what next steps you need to take to put this new system into action.

Do you need to create dedicated time in your calendar to complete the list of tasks that only you can do?

Who do you need to hire?

Do current systems and processes need to be updated?

Are there things you need to cancel or subscriptions or systems you need to downgrade to a free version, for example, now you've streamlined your work tasks?

MONEY MAGNET TIP:

The 3-D system only works if you communicate it to your staff and contractors, set boundaries, expectations and deadlines and stick to the plan! If you find yourself going off track, taking on tasks you've previously delegated or dumped or you're tempted to throw in the towel and do everything yourself, keep in mind, that when you work in the areas of the business that make you money, it's one of the fastest ways to unlock your earning potential.

Your personal/business SWOT analysis

If you're in a bit of a business slump or so used to doing ALL the jobs that you no longer know what you're good at, consider doing a personal SWOT analysis.

Focusing on what you're good at in business and outsourcing the rest can help you unlock your earning potential. Here's an exercise to help you identify your strengths and expertise. How can you leverage what you're good at and overcome obstacles to help your business grow?

Strengths

1. What are you naturally good at, and what comes easily to you?

2. What are you qualified to do (think formal skills, education)?

3. What do others think you're good at or see as your strengths? Reach out to three friends or colleagues and ask.

4. What values do you believe in that set you apart?

5. What's your most outstanding achievement?

6. Write a list of your top twenty connections, those people that you

can call on to help you.

Weaknesses

1. What tasks do you avoid doing? Consider where you need more confidence or competence.

2. Do you have any habits that will impact your business? For example, you need to be more focused, you're always running late or you find it hard to manage a team.

3. Ask your friends if they believe you have any specific weaknesses or where your personality or skill set might make you vulnerable.

4. What do you fear the most about business?

Opportunities

1. What's happening in your industry right now? Are there any market trends, both positive and negative, that you can leverage?

2. Are there tech or updated systems and processes that can help save you time and money?

3. Review your network; how can your network help market your business?

4. Think about your customers – what are they asking for; what do they want more of; what do they need help with? Is there a service or product void you can fill?

5. What events, business groups or new networks can you join to promote your business?

6. Is there a new market you have yet to try?

7. Are you checking in to see if you can help your former clients?

8. Speak to your team and get their input on any opportunities.

Threats

1. What's your business style? Are you a risk taker or risk-averse?

2. How's your cash flow? Do you need to make improvements?

3. What's your succession plan? What happens if you get sick or can't work?

4. Are there external circumstances from the economy, technology or market trends that might impact your business?

5. Does your business face any obstacles?

6. Consider your weaknesses. Do these lead to a threat to your business?

Momentum

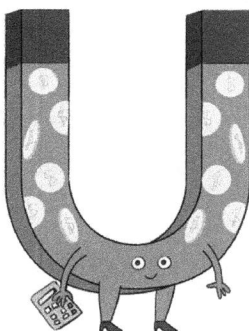

Chapter 16

Bringing it All Together

'A little progress each day adds up to BIG results!'

Justine McLean

There's nothing like a good quote. That perfect one-liner that gets you thinking about all the possibilities. And, if you've ever attended one of my workshops or masterclasses or followed me on socials, you'd definitely have heard a few of them – maybe even the one above.

But this one, *A little progress each day adds up to BIG results!* (or my other favourite, *consistency equals progress*), particularly resonates with me. I'm a bit of a perfectionist, an all-or-nothing kind of gal. If I can't do all the things and do them all well immediately, why bother at all?

Over the years, especially when I'm confronted with something that seems too big or overwhelming, or the perfectionist in me wants the all-or-nothing result, I remind myself that I don't need to be perfect or even right all the time. I certainly don't need to achieve everything I set out to accomplish in a week, a month or even six months.

But, I need consistency to get from where I am now to where I want to go.

I need to keep showing up and doing what needs to be done to help me and my business succeed.

So, as you embark on this journey to increase your financial literacy and become a business money magnet^{TM}, remember that it's all about consistency.

MONEY MAGNET TIP:

Keep showing up, and do one small thing every day, even if you fail – because pretty soon, all of those little actions will add up to big progress.

There's no such thing as 'set and forget' in business

How often have you heard someone refer to their business as their baby?

Over the years, I've heard all sorts of arguments for and against referring to a business as a baby, from "your business shouldn't depend on you, so it's not your baby", to a perceived inability to relinquish control if you refer to your business as a baby – and of course, the emotion over logic argument, that if you refer to your business as a baby, then you won't be able to make tough business decisions.

Now, if we were all logic and no emotion, those statements make a lot of sense. And while I know that words matter, in reality, we're all too smart to get sucked into the notion that our business is like our literal child. So, if you want to call your business your baby, I say have at it!

The reference makes a lot of sense. When you set out on the parenting journey (I'm talking about real-life children here) you have little clue what to expect. No matter how many parenting books you read or how much advice you get from everyone around you, the reality is that you're often just making it up as you go. You want to nurture and grow your tiny human, want only the best for them, and hope they'll succeed. While you know you need to take care of them when they're young, you also know that your job is to create a robust and independent individual who can eventually care for themselves.

And that's a little like your business.

But the comparison ends there because, at the heart of it, your business is an investment, an asset that you may sell at some point. And, while there's nothing wrong with being attached to your business, to create a profitable and sustainable business, you need to recognise that your business is an entity, a commodity, one that you want to grow to its full potential but one that you can mould and change to suit your circumstances and season of life too.

That's why there is no such thing as set and forget when it comes to business, which goes double for the business money. So, as you look at your business in its entirety and begin to make decisions about the way forward, it's essential to understand that your business will grow and change often. What worked two years ago might not work today or six months from now because you change, the economy changes, technology changes, thought leadership changes and your ideal client might change, too.

So, as you decide on your way forward and begin implementing some of the business money tools in this book, remember that you will need to adjust your plans as your business grows and use varying tools and strategies at different times to achieve the desired outcome.

And that's why it's crucial to increase your financial literacy so you can...

Become your own business consultant!

There's nothing I love more than working with a client as we scan through every aspect of their business. From the marketing to the finances, the offers to the operation, the best way to get more customers and how to nurture those existing clients.

Taking a helicopter view of your business is fun. But for a lot of business owners, it can be easier to hire a coach or consultant to help with a business review. While calling in an expert and seeing your business through someone else's lens is a great idea, I hope you'll become your own business consultant by implementing what you learn in this book.

The consultant's hat or CEO day

I put the consultant's hat on (or take a CEO day, as it's also commonly known) at least twice each year; once at the start of the calendar year and the other at the beginning of the financial year. While I look at my numbers weekly, taking that more comprehensive view of business helps me decide on my priorities over the next six months. More importantly, it also helps me see where to make strategic changes.

If you've ever got to the end of the year and wondered what the new year has in store for you and your business, or you know something is missing in the business but can't put your finger on the problem or the solution, then step back and take that helicopter view. Pull your business apart and put it back together again. I've made some of my best decisions while working through this process.

Here's what I do when I take a wholesale look at my business and become my own consultant. It's similar to setting financial goals, but there are a few differences.

The process starts with understanding where you and your business are at right now. Set aside a couple of hours, grab a pen and paper and ask yourself these questions.

I'll always think about a specific period in business – the last quarter, half year or year – as I undertake this task. Doing this will help you clarify where you're at and illuminate where you want to go.

- What's been working in the business?

- What do you enjoy doing, and what do you want to do more?

- Where's your time best spent?

- What areas of the business didn't work or aren't working?

- What do you want to do less of?

- What needs to change?

- Are your current goals still relevant?

Once you have the answers to those questions, it's time to dig a little deeper:

- Think about your business/life balance. When you understand what success means for this next season of life and business, what do you need to change to help you achieve your success goal?

- How are the business numbers stacking up? Review all the numbers here, specifically:

  - The turnover and net profit – review your profit and loss statement.

  - The business cash flow.

- ○ Your cost of doing business.

  - ○ The social media numbers. Also consider your engagement; what's working, what isn't?

- How does your ascension model or suite of products and service offers stack up? Does it need a review or revamp?

- Does your current pricing structure work?

- Think about your ideal clients and conduct a customer analysis:

  - ○ Do you know who your ideal client is, and has that changed since you started your business?

  - ○ What's your lead generation strategy?

  - ○ How many new leads are you adding to your ecosystem each month?

  - ○ What's your customer conversion rate, and does this need improving?

  - ○ Do you have a customer retention strategy? Does it need a re-vamp, and how many of your former customers are choosing to work with you again?

  - ○ What are your mailing list numbers? Are you nurturing your mailing list with regular newsletters?

Once you've answered those questions, you can then review your internal processes.

- Do you have all of the business processes documented?

- Do you have good systems in place?

- Where can you improve?

- What changes can you make to increase efficiency?

Next, conduct a review of staffing including any consultants or free-lancers you use.

- Is it time to increase staff, outsource, or cut back?

As you work through this process, you'll have a better understanding of where you need to make changes within your business. Each time you conduct a review and become your own consultant, you'll gain more clarity about your business and what you need to do to build a business you'll love.

Review and reset – the crucial metrics to consider

When you pop on the consultant's hat, if you want to focus purely on the business from a financial perspective, here's what you should consider measuring.

- **Revenue:** The amount of money the business brings in or total turnover.

- **Gross Profit Margin:** The proportion of revenue remaining after subtracting the cost of goods sold.

- **Net Profit Margin:** The revenue amount remaining after all expenses are subtracted.

- **Customer Acquisition Cost:** What it costs to acquire a new customer, including marketing, advertising and sales expenses.

- **Expense Ratio:** The ratio of expenses to revenue; this figure helps to understand the business's cost structure. To calculate, divide the total operating expenses by the gross revenue.

- **Inventory Turnover:** A measure of how quickly the business sells its stock or inventory.

- **Debt-to-equity Ratio:** The ratio of debt to equity shows how much debt a business has compared to its assets. To calculate, you will need to add up all of the business debts (short-term loans, long-term loans and any other debts – you will find these on the balance sheet) and then divide them by the equity in the business.

- **Lifetime value of a customer:** The estimated revenue a customer will generate for the business over their relationship.

- **Average Order Value:** The average amount of money spent per order by your customers. To calculate, divide the total revenue by the total number of orders.

- **Return on Investment (ROI):** The return on investment in marketing, operations, or any other business activity.

- **Employee Turnover Rate:** How often are your employees leaving the business?

- **Customer Satisfaction:** A measure of customers' satisfaction with the business's products or services. You can gauge this through a post-service survey or review, for example.

- **Conversion Rate:** How many of your website visitors completed a desired action, such as making a purchase or downloading a lead magnet, or how many discovery calls resulted in a sale of your product or service?

- **Traffic:** The number of visitors to the business's website or physical location. You can look at both unique and returning visitors.

- **Engagement:** The number of followers on social media and other platforms who engaged or took action on your content.

- **Market Share:** How much of the market does your business currently serve?

YOUR FINANCIAL CHECKUP CALENDAR

Every Week

- Set aside a money 'hour of power' – Money Monday or Finance Friday

  - Pay bills, wages and any other business expenses.

  - Invoice and follow-up overdue payments.

  - Complete or check transfers for savings and tax.

  - Update your cash flow, check your P&L and make sure your business is on track.

  - Review an expense line and see where you can save.

  - For more money ideas head on back to chapter 14.

Every Month

- Reconcile your cloud accounting software or bank statement.

- Check the business cash flow – are you on track?

- Review the P&L.

- Update all of the numbers you're keeping track of – from cash in the bank to social media and everything else on your list.

- Take a look at your business goals – what do you still need to do to achieve them?

- Talk to your bookkeeper, accountant or business money mentor.

Every Quarter

- Book in your CEO Day – put on the consultant's hat and take a deep dive into the business.

- Plan the next quarter.

- Review, finalise and lodge any relevant compliance.

- Pay your superannuation obligations.

- Celebrate the wins!

Every Six Months

- Review your offers and your prices!

Every Year

- Finalise your accounts, do annual checks and reviews and send your business financials off to a qualified accountant so your taxes can be prepared.

- Check in with your accountant – review the year and get their advice for the year ahead.

- Do a deep dive into your business:

  - Decide on what success looks like for you in the year ahead.

  - Review your offers and your prices!

  - Finalise your goals for the new business year.

- Update your calendar with all of the relevant dates for the year ahead including your weekly money hour of power, your CEO and planning days, compliance due dates, major bill due dates and your pricing reviews.

Is it time to scale your business?

No matter what stage you're at in business, at some point on the journey, you'll think about scaling your business. There could be many reasons:

- You no longer want to do everything yourself, and it's time to bring on a team.

- You've created something that's in demand.

- You want to diversify and bring in a new income stream.

- You want to make more money.

While that list is not exhaustive, these are the main reasons business owners choose to grow. So, naturally, the next logical question is when to take the next step and how to make that happen.

In my experience, whether you're growing from a solopreneur and taking on a contractor or moving into a new turnover bracket and need to take on multiple new staff and invest in equipment and office space, three areas of business need to be ship-shape to make the transition a success: finances, systems and processes and staff. No matter how big or small your business is, these three pillars are the key to sustainable growth.

The finances

The good news is that you can scale your business at any time! But to do it successfully, you must have a handle on the finances, be making a profit, have great systems and processes in place, and have clearly defined job descriptions for each new or prospective team member. If you can tick all of these boxes, you're good to go!

Now, if you're not ticking these boxes, you'll need to go back to basics, look at each of the three pillars and determine what you need to do to move forward sustainably. After all, the last thing you want to do is scale your business, find yourself in debt and then have to take a step back. Retrenching staff is never fun.

Everything you need to do to create a profitable business is in this book, so put on the consultant's hat and work out what you need to do to take the next steps to profitability.

Systems and processes

Improving systems and processes is easy; it's about getting all of the stuff, those day-to-day repetitive tasks, out of your head and onto 'paper'. Head back to chapter eight to learn more about developing best practice systems and processes.

Team and contractors

When it comes to employing a team, one of the biggest problems for business owners and CEOs alike is the inability to let go because no one quite 'gets it' like you do. Hands up if you're guilty of that? Yep, me too!

However, the key to sustainable growth is not only your ability to trust someone else to do the work, but also to have clearly defined job descriptions and tasks for each team member. It's also vital to employ the right people for each job.

When we employ that first team member, we often choose an assistant or VA or someone with one particular skill set, like a social media manager. And they come into the business to do that specific job. But, as the business grows, we often find ourselves delegating tasks to our VA or social media manager that don't fit that person's skill set.

A great example is my client Susan.

Susan's business was growing fast and her VA, Michelle, originally employed to work 10 hours a week doing the administrative tasks, was now doing the admin and social media. So, when Susan no longer had time to look after the account payments, Michelle was the next logical choice. Michelle was already in the business, had a great working relationship with Susan and needed the extra money. But what started as paying a few bills soon led to looking after all the business money stuff, including the bookkeeping and quarterly tax returns. Michelle was out of her depth.

Pretty soon the books were a mess, Michelle was stressed and unhappy, and Susan was frustrated because things were no longer being done properly. Susan had to step back in, clean up the mess, and take back the work herself. Her focus was no longer where it needed to be and business growth soon stalled. I've seen it too many times!

For successful business growth, choose the right person for each role in the business. When interviewing, share that you'll likely look to grow the business and ask them if they can do x or y or if they have skills outside of the job they're applying for. That way, you'll instantly gauge their feelings about additional work or upskilling. If you already have team members, the same applies.

The bottom line is that if you want to grow your business, you need to be able to delegate so everything doesn't rely on **you**, because you will become the bottleneck and stop any business growth in its tracks!

MONEY MAGNET TIP:

Remember, your team is one of your most valuable business assets, and a happy team can be the key to helping you achieve your goals.

And while we're talking, team...

Behind every successful small business is a solid and cohesive team, and the best business owners recognise that success is intricately tied to their team members' collective efforts and dedication.

Building a motivated and cohesive team can propel your business towards achieving its goals.

Here are my tips for fostering a successful team and providing them with the necessary support to thrive. It's all about bringing them along on the business journey.

Define a clear vision

Step one is to establish a clear and compelling vision for your business. Share your long-term goals and communicate how each team member contributes to the bigger picture. When employees understand the purpose and direction of their work, they feel a sense of ownership and motivation to contribute to the business's overall success.

Encourage open communication

Effective communication is the lifeblood of any business. Encourage open and honest communication channels among team members. Everyone should feel comfortable sharing their thoughts, ideas, and concerns.

You'll be surprised at what you can achieve when you foster an environment where collaboration is encouraged, and diverse perspectives are valued. A staple in my business is the regular team meetings and brainstorming sessions. Those work-in-progress meetings and feedback loop opportunities are excellent ways to facilitate effective communication.

Foster a culture of trust, inclusivity and respect

Trust and respect are the foundation of a successful team. So treat your team members with dignity, appreciation, fairness and respect.

Encourage collaboration and teamwork while also celebrating individual achievements. Offer opportunities for professional growth and development and allow team members to improve their skills and feel valued for their contributions. When team members feel respected and trusted, they are more likely to go the extra mile for the business's success.

Diverse perspectives and expertise

One of the most significant benefits of having a team is the diverse range of perspectives and expertise they bring to the table. Each team member possesses unique skills and knowledge.

So, ask your team to evaluate and enhance existing systems and processes. When you're choosing a team, keep an open mind. While employing team members with shared values is vital, considering diverse perspectives is also a great idea.

When an area of your business needs improving, ask your team first; they usually have the best ideas and can help you implement innovative solutions, too.

Delegate with confidence

As a business leader, trusting your team and delegating tasks lightens your workload and empowers your team.

Have clearly defined roles and job descriptions. Then choose the right person for the job! You'll need to identify the strengths and skills of your prospective team members so you can be sure from the get-go that they can complete the tasks assigned and grow with the business as you scale.

Remember, when you delegate, provide clear instructions and offer guidance when needed, but always trust your team to deliver quality results. And, if there's a problem, address it early.

Encourage collaboration and teamwork

Success is seldom achieved in isolation. That's why it's crucial to encourage collaboration and teamwork among your employees.

Build a supportive environment where team members can share knowledge, exchange ideas, and work together towards common objectives. The best ways to improve collaboration and teamwork are often through team-building activities, such as group projects, team outings or development days.

Increased efficiency

Small business is all about efficiency because resources are often in short supply. One of the best ways to increase efficiency is through effective systems and processes; the best way to create these is to make the process organic and ongoing.

Ask your team to help shape your processes and suggest systems to improve efficiency and save time or money. Your team is bound to have a different take on how to do the day-to-day tasks in the business. Their insights could help achieve a smoother, more streamlined operation and increase profits, too.

Provide recognition and rewards

We all like to feel we're doing a good job, so recognising and rewarding your team's achievements will do wonders for your business. Celebrate milestones or acknowledge exceptional performance.

Rewards can take various forms; you can offer bonuses, incentives, days off or public recognition, but remember, recognition doesn't always have to be material. A simple 'thank you' or a genuine appreciation email can go a long way in boosting team morale.

Foster a healthy work-life balance

Offering flexibility, promoting wellness initiatives and being interested in your team's well-being helps them feel supported and can improve productivity and loyalty.

Strive to create a work environment that supports a healthy work-life balance for your team members.

During Covid, many team members could work from home and enjoy the extra time that gave them with their loved ones. While it may not be practical to have your team working from home one hundred percent of the time, think about ways to encourage them to find a more balanced approach to work.

Building and nurturing a solid team is one of the secrets to growing your business. By defining a clear vision, fostering open communication, cultivating trust, and providing recognition, you can bring your team along for the ride and propel your business towards achieving its goals. Remember, a motivated and engaged team is the driving force behind sustainable and profitable growth and success.

Celebrate the wins!

As you bring all the business puzzle pieces together, especially as you get a handle on the business finances, ensure you celebrate your wins! And not just the big, flashy stuff but the weekly and even daily wins!

- Maybe you stopped working when you said you would – there's a win!

- You finished and delivered a client project early – there's a win!

- You spent an hour weekly on the business money for the last four weeks – there's a win, too!

No matter how big or small the wins, make sure you take some time to congratulate yourself on your hard work and achievement. Because when you leave the celebrating for later, your business quickly becomes a grind and there's nothing to look forward to, so decide on a win for each week and get celebrating!

Chapter 17

Staying On the Path to Profit

'Option A is not available. So, let's kick the shit out of option B!'

Sheryl Sandberg

Profit is addictive! Once you've experienced your first taste of business profit, I guarantee it's something you'll want to see repeated again and again. Because no matter what success looks like for you in your business right now, the ability to achieve your unique goals and do it profitably allows you more freedom as you move forward.

Watching my net profit and profit account increase in value each month motivates me to stay on the path to profit. However, for many business owners, staying profitable month after month is just plain hard work. What was working last month isn't working this month; economic circumstances outside your control are starting to bite, it's not business as usual, and you can't work out why.

And while Sheryl Sandberg is on to something, here are my tips for staying on the path to profit.

Don't let them forget about you

If you've been in business for a while, you've probably heard about the 80/20 rule, aka the Pareto Principle. While the 80/20 rule applies to many different aspects of business, in a nutshell, it asserts that 80 percent of all outcomes or outputs result from 20 percent of all causes or inputs. In other words, prioritise the 20 percent that will give you the best results.

When it comes to business profit, 80 percent of your profit is likely to come from 20 percent of your customers. So, identifying that 20 percent and maximising the time you work with them is an easy first step to staying on the path to profit.

While the idea seems pretty straightforward, the reality can be more complex, and that's largely because, just like us, our customers are often guilty of looking for the shiny, next-best thing and they forget all about us. Sure, you provided an excellent service and have the testimonial to prove it, but that business over there offers something similar, or the on-trend influencer says it's good, so, your customer is off, out of your orbit and working with someone else before you know what's happened.

Naturally, as business owners, we expect our happy customers to come back for more at some point, so we don't tend to chase them. And, as the busyness of business takes hold, we often forget our 'old' customers altogether. Instead, we're on the lookout for the next new customer.

But, as we've already covered, getting that new customer can be expensive. When you put that into the context of the 80/20 rule, you have to wonder why you'd even bother chasing after someone new when you've got potential sales sitting on the table ready for the taking.

Moral of the story? *Don't let your customers forget about you!*

Remind them you're still here. Whether following up about the work you've just completed, suggesting another way you can work together or creating a special VIP offer for your preferred clients, think about what you can do to keep customers coming back for more.

If you want to hold on to your 20 percent, you need to ask!

Let your current clients know you're open for work. If you don't tell them, how will they know?

Let them know how you can help them. Suggest one thing you can do to make their life more manageable right now.

If you don't have them on your email list, add them, with consent of course and according to the GDPR laws in your region. Then, make sure you nurture your list. Don't just reach out when you're selling and need more money; share tips and strategies to help your customers when you're not working together. You'll turn regular clients into loyal, raving fans when you stay engaged and keep serving them for free.

And, if you don't have a list, but know that your clients follow you on socials, then share your monthly specials or let them know you've got the capacity to help them; 'I have one spot left this month!', for example.

If your former clients don't need your services right now, share that you're open for work and ask them to recommend you. Just because they don't need your services doesn't mean you can't ask them for a helping hand. Consider offering a referral fee for a new client as an incentive.

A final word on asking. Ask your happy clients for a testimonial or Google review. When you get those testimonials, store them in one place and use them in your marketing!

Diversify your income streams and increase profits

You've probably heard business owners chatting about their multiple income streams. It's better known as diversifying and simply means creating new or varied income sources to help your business grow and adapt to changing market conditions.

My company, for example, has various income streams, including online programs and courses, 1:1 and group coaching, speaking and workshop presentations, retreats and events, affiliate income, and the Secrets of Successful Business Podcast.

In 2016, my business also included an income stream offering book-keeping and compliance services. However, I sold that income stream in February 2023 for a large profit and I'm yet to replace it, but I'm always looking for new ways to increase income and profit.

There are many benefits when diversifying your business income. Not only is it a lucrative way to make more money, but it can also help reduce risk and allow you to discover fresh opportunities.

For my client, Chrissie, diversifying business income meant unlocking additional revenue sources, and that saved her business from extinction as the full impact of the pandemic took hold. Chrissie ran a business that had several income streams, but over the years before COVID-19, she'd let most of them sit idle because, by far, her biggest money earner was event and wedding planning.

In Australia, the pandemic meant large gatherings, including weddings, were off the table, so, literally overnight, Chrissie lost 100 percent of her business. With no way of making a living out of her traditional services, we decided to look at all of the dormant income streams in her business. Fortunately, and with only a tiny amount of work, we could resurrect a few of those income streams.

Chrissie already had a track record in design, mentoring and coaching so she used her existing list and knowledge to jump on the virtual bandwagon. Within months, Chrissie was earning again, able to re-engage her team of contractors and survive what would have otherwise been the end of her business.

While that's an extreme example of how diversifying can help your business, it shows the power of having multiple business income streams.

Depending on your industry and skillset, adding additional income streams to your business can also help you enter new markets, attract new customers, strengthen customer relationships, and enhance loyalty.

Diversification in business can also contribute to long-term sustainability and it can help you stay on the path to profit.

How can you diversify your business income streams?

First off, make sure you understand your customers. Consider reaching out to your existing and potential customers via surveys or asking for feedback. When you speak with your customers, ask them about their evolving needs and preferences and analyse their behaviour to help you identify areas for expansion or new income streams. By putting your customers and their needs first, you can often find the right opportunities to organically grow and diversify your business.

Next, explore the wider market or industry you're currently working in to identify trends, customer demands, and untapped opportunities. Speak to other business owners in your field, attend seminars or industry events and see what you can uncover. Sometimes the simplest thing can lead to the most surprising result!

Adding a new income stream

Before you choose to add a new income stream to your business, it's also vital to know your strengths and weaknesses and your business's strengths and weaknesses. There's no point adding to an already full plate or taking on something you won't like doing, so be honest with yourself before taking the next step. Leverage your strengths and identify new revenue sources aligning with your business.

Keep in mind that you don't have to go it alone when adding a new source of income to your business. Consider collaborating with partnerships or other businesses who share similar values or where you can expand your product and service offerings with little effort; affiliate marketing is a great example.

You might also like to think about introducing or exploring new technologies, distribution channels, and expertise, too. The introduction of AI, for example, has given copywriters an opportunity to explore the platform, discover the best way to leverage the technology and then share how to use it with their clients and peers.

As you explore new income streams, it's important to evaluate and manage associated risks before you choose to pull the trigger. Consider financial viability, scalability, and potential impacts on your existing revenue streams; there's no point adding a new income stream that will cannibalise your main income earner, for example. When you decide to add a new income stream, start with small experiments and pilot projects to minimise risks before you make the decision to scale.

MONEY MAGNET TIP:

The business landscape is constantly evolving, so it's essential to stay nimble and responsive to changes in the market and your customers' needs. Always monitor each income stream regularly by tracking the income, associated expenses and profit. I like to create separate profit and loss statements for each income source so I can review the profitability of each income stream and then decide what I want to continue and what's not working.

Examples of business income streams:

- Events, workshops and retreats.

- Start and monetise a podcast.

- White label a product that's already working well for your business.

- Add additional services to your existing offers – consider packaging up services or filling the gaps in your product or service value ladder.

- Add virtual services.

- Start selling online.

- Drop-ship services.

- Collaborate with like-minded business owners.

- Pursue affiliate opportunities.

- Sub-lease your space or rent equipment.

- Coaching and mentoring.

Going for the quick wins!

Sometimes, staying on the path to profit, especially when cash flow is tight, means investing in some quick wins.

The quick wins are those things that are short term, one-offs and that create an immediate cash injection for your business. These are also services that require minimum input in time, resources and effort from you. They're also useful if you want to test a new income stream or bring a new service to the market and get feedback from clients, too.

MONEY MAGNET TIP:

Think out of the box! And remember, you don't need to add any of these quick wins as regular income streams; pick and choose what will give you the maximum return for the least effort and do that.

---

35 ways to make more money in your business

1. Explore opportunities to get paid to speak. Deliver a keynote as a guest expert speaker at industry conferences or trade shows.

2. Offer a webinar or masterclass.

3. Reach out to business owners who have groups and offer to be their monthly expert.

4. Create and sell digital products and templates or courses related to your expertise or industry – think of those things you use often or questions that come up all the time and create something to fill the void.

5. Increase prices on a select product or service.

6. Run a promotion or a limited-time offer – get rid of that obsolete product or overstock.

7. Upsell and cross-sell.

8. Get involved in community events.

9. Throw some money into advertising.

10. Consider an old-fashioned service swap – you'll save money on expenses, but it will cost you your time.

11. Check out the local, state and federal government website for grants or seek funding.

12. Offer new or bespoke services to existing customers – yep back to the 80/20 rule here.

13. Use cash-back sites when you buy online – great for both business and personal expenses too.

14. Expand your target market.

15. Collaborate with like-minded business owners – share the risk, the reward and your audiences for maximum impact.

16. Try local area marketing to reach more potential customers close to home.

17. Offer limited premium or VIP services with added value as a high-ticket offer.

18. Add a consulting or coaching income stream to your business. Offer ad-hoc mentoring or coaching services to other professionals with less experience.

19. Sell merchandise or branded products or provide white label solutions for other businesses.

20. Implement a subscription or membership model.

21. Offer discounts for bulk purchases.

22. Partner with influencers or brand ambassadors.

23. Create and monetise content through a blog, podcast, or YouTube channel – consider sponsored posts.

24. Host events or retreats.

25. Offer payment plans or financing options to attract those 'on the fence' clients.

26. Provide add-on or quick turnaround services for an additional fee.

27. Bundle products or services to make them appear more attractive or better value.

28. Sell advertising space on your website or in your newsletters. Some business owners now have a subscription-only newsletter where the recipient gets access to exclusive content for a fee.

29. Explore new distribution channels or partnerships.

30. Expand your geographical reach through online sales or international partnerships.

31. Participate in paid market research.

32. Create a loyalty program to reward repeat customers.

33. Offer corporate training or consulting services.

34. Write a book.

35. Provide affiliate programs and ask selected partners to promote

your products or services for a commission or launch a referral program to encourage word-of-mouth marketing.

Learn to navigate the challenges

Business, just like life, has constant ups and downs; some we can control, and some we can't. Whether it's external factors like interest rate increases, elections, natural disasters or seasonal sale time, or something internal like staffing issues, a change in market focus, or a link on your website that's broken, being in business is about navigating the challenges so you can stay on the path to profit and build those resilience muscles too.

As business owners, we like to think that we've got a handle on everything, but there will be a time in your business when things don't go your way. For many business owners, the first indication that things aren't right shows up in the finances: the sales aren't coming through, the bank balance is looking a little sad, downward trends are showing in the reports, or the cost of doing business has increased exponentially. Profit might be at an all-time low.

The key to navigating those challenges is to be astute enough to see the downturn or issue as it happens and implement appropriate strategies and changes quickly. So, if the business finances are moving in the wrong direction or it's clear that something needs to improve, here are a few strategies to consider when things aren't going your way.

First, assess the situation and review the financial statements like the profit and loss, the budget, and cash flow projections to determine where the problems exist. By comparing where you are now to where you were a few weeks or months ago, you'll immediately know what needs to change.

For example, if the cost of doing business has increased and is draining the funds, you might need to cut costs. Spend some time identifying areas where you can reduce expenses, make changes to minimise waste and increase profitability.

Take a look at increasing revenue. Implement a strategy to increase sales; offer a quick win, sale or promotion, create a new offer or expand the existing product line, retire things that are no longer working, diversify revenue streams or pursue new marketing opportunities via collabs or service swaps.

It's also an excellent time to improve cash flow management. If you don't have a cash flow management strategy, it's time to implement one. If you do have a cash flow strategy, consider how to increase the cash inflows and decrease outflows. Tighten payment terms and ask your suppliers for extra time to pay, for example.

If all else fails, or you're unsure what to do, seek professional help. Consider hiring an accountant, CFO or business money coach to provide expert advice and support on financial management.

MONEY MAGNET TIP:

Turning around a struggling business requires patience, persistence, and a commitment to making the necessary changes. The earlier you take action, the more likely you are to achieve success and get back on the path to profit.

How to bounce back from business disappointment

Dealing with disappointment in business can be challenging. Often, the immediate reaction is to want to give up or question why you're doing what you're doing.

But, when those inevitable disappointments occur, before you spiral into negative thinking, self-doubt or worse, consider throwing in the towel –

take a moment to consider why you started your business in the first place. Was it to spend more time with your family, to showcase a fantastic service to the world that you know will change lives, or because you wanted to work for yourself on your terms? Understanding why you started your business and drawing on that in the downtimes can be all that's needed to get you over the hurdle you're facing; that and a good bit of strategy, too.

In addition to remembering your why, one of the best ways to deal with business disappointment is to get real and be honest with yourself. Ask yourself if your business is still serving you and if you want to continue, if the answer is no, it might be time to stop and consider selling or winding things down.

But, if the answer is a resounding yes, then move forward using some of these strategies to help you bounce back:

- **Reframe your thinking:** A healthy business mindset is essential! You can choose how you react to any situation, so start by viewing disappointment as a learning opportunity and reframe it positively. Focus on what you can do differently in the future and what you can take away from the experience. There's always a lesson to be learned when disappointment hits.

- **Take some time out or schedule a break:** Sometimes, the white space is where the magic happens, so if the business has got you down, consider taking time out to process what's happening, deal with your emotions and recharge. Taking a break, even a day or two, can help you gain a fresh perspective and return with renewed energy.

- **Ask for help:** Be bold about asking for help, especially if you're still finding your feet or trying to figure out what to do next. Talk to trusted friends, family members, business colleagues or a business expert about what's happening in the business. Sometimes it's those people outside the business who can offer a fresh perspective and provide the smartest strategy to manage the way forward.

- **Get real:** Take a complete and honest look at all areas of your business and identify where the problems exist. If it's a one-off incident like an unhappy customer, that's easy to solve. However, if an issue keeps repeating itself, like no money in the bank to pay the bills, for example, you need to investigate the why. What's happening with the finances, and how can you plug that leaky bucket? Once you understand where the problem is, you'll have a better chance of fixing the issue.

- **Set some goals and create a plan:** There's nothing better than a good planning session, and when you need to bounce back from disappointment, often the best way to do that is to develop a plan for moving forward. Start by identifying the problem or issue, then decide what your business would look like if you solved the problem. What steps must you take to get you from where you are now to where you want to go? Map them out, put some dates around them and step forward.

- **Stay motivated:** Surround yourself with positive business role models and people outside of business who boost your mindset: the givers, not the takers. Try a nature walk to clear your head or engage in activities you enjoy. And when it comes to those business goals, set small, achievable goals to help keep you motivated and focused on your success journey.

> **MONEY MAGNET TIP:**
>
> Setbacks and disappointments are a normal part of running a business. The key is to learn from them, be resilient, and stay focused on your goals. You can bounce back and achieve your desired success with persistence and determination.

Watch out for scams

As business technology improves, so do the business scams, from the links in text messages to those official-looking emails to even the most subtle tricks employed by businesses and scammers alike to take your money.

Anyone can fall victim to a scam and I've seen how detrimental the fallout can be for a business, the cash flow and profit. So as scams evolve, staying on top of the latest information and being vigilant for red flags is essential. If it's too good to be true, that's probably about right. Here are some business scams to watch out for:

Email interception scams

This is a sophisticated scam where bank account details on an email or invoice attached to an email are altered by the scammer rather than the sender. I first heard of this scam when a lawyer I was working with reached out to double check the bank account for a deposit transfer. It seemed odd at the time, but the lawyer assured me that the scam was on the rise. Hackers typically target emails where large money transfers are requested, house deposits for example, and then alter details with the receiver of the email none the wiser.

While I'd heard of account details on invoices being altered by people sending invoices and was always in the habit of checking bank details on a new invoice against bank details I'd used in the past, this scam took me a little by surprise. Fortunately, in this case, it all checked out and no one lost any money, but it's certainly worth staying vigilant whenever emails arrive that ask for money.

Rule of thumb: it's best to be on the safe side and always double check bank details, particularly when paying a new supplier or if the supplier details you've been using for a while have changed.

Impersonation scams

As a registered BAS agent, one of my jobs is to process and lodge quarterly Business Activity Statements with the local tax authority. These statements report earnings and expenses to the government and also outline any tax collected by the business and due to the tax office. Once the BAS return is lodged, the tax department produces communication outlining the pay amount and details.

While it's challenging to fabricate these reports, there was a very convincing scam a few years back where someone pretending to be an agent from the tax department contacted business owners by phone and advised them of outstanding tax debts. It was around the time the BAS payments were due, so at face value, it made sense. However, what I knew, and what my clients needed to know was that the tax department would rarely reach out on the phone. Instead, they'd send a message through a secure portal.

In this scam, the 'tax agent' asked business owners to pay their outstanding tax debt over the phone using their credit card. Unfortunately, some business owners were victims of the scam and lost a lot of money; their tax debt was still outstanding.

In another recent example of an impersonation scam, a 'bank employee' contacted my client and advised that odd transactions had occurred on their company account. Initially, the 'bank employee' asked my client to be vigilant and watch for anything untoward. Then, over several days, the same 'bank employee' would reach out to check in, always claiming that the 'bank' was blocking these fraudulent transactions.

Naturally, my client was thankful that the 'bank' was being so diligent and helpful.

After several days, the 'bank' contacted my client to say that the potential fraud had escalated. The 'bank' advised that it was best to create another online account and transfer the company funds to that account; they'd even wait on the phone while my client created the account.

The 'bank employee' then asked for the new account details, told my client to stay on the line and advised that they'd check at their end to ensure everything was okay. However, while my client sat on hold, the alleged bank employee was tapping into the new account and, once the funds from the company account were deposited, took those funds and transferred them elsewhere. While my client eventually recouped the funds, it took months of angst and back and forth with the bank to resolve the fraud.

While these two scams were indeed sophisticated and very elaborate in their setup and in the latter case in the patience shown by the scammer, we've all been on the end of a scam call.

The other day, I had a call from the 'credit card fraud department' asking if I'd just sent $990 to New Zealand. Rather than believing them at face value, I asked which card was used, my Visa or Mastercard. I don't have a Visa card so they had a 50 percent chance of getting it right. When they advised that it was my Visa card I knew it was a scam call.

Even when I relayed this, undeterred, the scammer continued, apologising and advising that she'd made a mistake and it was indeed my

Mastercard. So naturally, I asked for the last four digits; the call was immediately disconnected.

The point here is that despite the government-run anti-scam centres and all the tech that should block these scams, there will always be scammers who call impersonating someone else. Remember, if a bank, the tax department or any other 'authority' calls you, they should never ask you to divulge your passwords, complete account details, or other sensitive details over the phone. If they've called you, the burden of proving they're legit falls on them.

To be extra vigilant, rather than provide any details over the phone, I always ask for phone and email contacts and then use a Google search to see if they're legit.

When in doubt, call the main reception number of the company or bank reaching out to you and check the authenticity of the call.

You're not obligated to share sensitive information over the phone or via email or text. And while you're likely too savvy to ever click on links, know that no legitimate organisation will ask you to transfer money or make a payment over the phone; there are many other secure ways to do this if the caller proves authentic.

Investment scams

Investment scams can be hard to spot but are on the increase worldwide. From offers to buy cryptocurrency or fake bonds or shares and even the odd MLM (multi-level marketing opportunity), if it's a get-rich-quick opportunity or a 'sure-bet', it could be a scam so always investigate before you buy in.

There are also less sophisticated scams, which are as simple as using a celebrity or influencer's image to endorse a product or service.

The bottom line is to refrain from investing or buying into the idea of fast money. While adding a potential 'good bet' as a business income stream is tempting, these often end in disaster. But, if you're tempted to take the plunge, do your due diligence and ensure you can afford to lose what you invest.

Convenience tricks

I can't call these a scam because they aren't, but every time you get roped into using a third party for a convenience payment, you are spending money you don't need to spend. There are two big ones here in Australia and likely similar ones worldwide.

To operate a business in Australia, you need an Australian Business Number (ABN) and they're free. The best place to register for an ABN is directly via the federal government website, so naturally, when you do an internet search for ABN, you'd think that the appropriate government website would hit the top of the search. Um, nope. Instead, many businesses are happy to register for an ABN on your behalf and these are the ones landing right at the top of the Google search.

Now, not only is this service costing you money, but you're also handing over your information to some random business who has nothing to do with the government. So, if you need to do any business registrations, go straight to the relevant government authority that's requested the registration and follow their guidelines.

The other convenience trick that really bugs me and one countless clients have lost money on over the years is the business name registration renewal.

If you live in Australia and have a business name you need to renew your business name registration every year. Usually, a few weeks before the registration is due, you'll get a bill in the post for the renewal. These third-party businesses will renew your business name on your behalf, so it's convenient, but it genuinely only saves you a few minutes of work – and will also cost you around three times the price of a regular renewal – so instead of costing $42AUD you'll be paying around $199AUD.

If you want to save some hard-earned cash, wait for the government authority (in Australia it's ASIC) to email you about your business name renewal and re-register using the links provided.

There are many more convenience tricks that busy business owners take advantage of, and if you're time-poor and you've got money to burn, then go for it. But I believe in running a lean business and keeping money in my pocket. So, stay vigilant and make smart, money-saving business choices to stay on the path to profit.

What is your contingency plan?

Do you have a contingency plan? Because often, the only way to stay on the path to profit is to know what to do when the unexpected happens.

As business owners, we always strive to deliver outstanding service and keep our customers coming back for more, all while making enough money to create the life we love. It often involves burning the candle at both ends, sleepless nights and minds that never really switch off. Over the years, I've discovered it's something that non-businesspeople rarely understand.

And while most of us think business 24/7, 365, only some create a contingency plan, just in case something goes awry.

I know first-hand the benefits of a good contingency plan because, in late 2022, I had to rely on it to keep my business going.

It was the October long weekend. On the Friday beforehand, I'd been to a day surgery for a routine procedure. It was one of those preventative procedures and, as I understood it, relatively straightforward. So, naturally, I expected to go home, rest over the weekend and be back to work on Tuesday. However, the next day, I felt awful. I'd cleaned the house that morning, probably not wise in hindsight, and felt tired and a little out of sorts – nothing a rest wouldn't cure.

But roll forward over the weekend, and I became extremely unwell. I didn't want a fuss so I waited until Tuesday to see the family doctor, but instead of getting some medicine and going back to work, I landed in the ER and spent the next 9 days in hospital with an infection.

Then, less than a month later, I was back in the hospital again, this time with transient global amnesia (TGA). Yes, it's as frightening as it sounds.

Over a period of a few months, I spent almost five weeks on the fringes of my business, not selling, not doing the day-to-day, not performing at my usual capacity. My business survived. Not only that, but we continued to make a profit. I was unwell but still had the luxury of taking time out. Why?

Because I had a solid contingency plan, plus some excellent staff.

What did my contingency plan look like?

Over many years in business, I'd set aside three months' expenses in a savings account. That means I did not have to worry about money if something went wrong, but I also knew that my business could operate for three months if it didn't make another cent during that period.

I had great systems and processes in place and a fantastic team. Everyone knew how to carry on, and if they had a question, the first port of call was the systems and procedures.

Should the worst happen, I also had a succession plan in place, one that my accountant and my husband were aware of. In this instance, the worst meant me being out of action for a few weeks, and one of my team members gladly stepped up and filled in. But, in case of a longer lasting emergency, I also have a business will in place, sharing my wishes about winding up the company and exactly how to do it.

We all like to think we're invincible, but inevitably, there will be a time in your business when you need to take some time out for a short while, a few months or completely. Think about your contingency plan and take it from someone who has been there; your business contingency is the friend you'll be thrilled you have on your team, just in case!

MONEY MAGNET TIP:

Start your contingency plan by thinking about the best way for the business to continue, if that's your desire, while you take some time out. Who do you want to lead? Do your current systems and processes support the business if you need to step away? Do you have an emergency fund that will sustain you?

Once you've got a plan in place, share it with key stakeholders and family and ensure you review your contingency plan at least once a year.

How do you know when it's time to sell?

As I've already shared, in February 2023, I sold off my business's book-keeping and compliance arm.

While selling that arm of my business had always been the plan 'at some stage', at the time, it wasn't on the immediate agenda. However, feeling exhausted and a little overwhelmed by running so many aspects of the company, I threw the idea out in a conversation with my hubby on a drive down to the south coast. We chatted about the possibility of selling and what it might look like and left it at that.

A week later, curiosity got the better of me. I wanted to know what my business was worth, so I contacted my accountant and asked him to value that area of the business.

Now, when you're running multiple businesses under a single entity, or if you've got multiple income streams in your business and think you might sell one or all of them at some point, setting things up correctly from the get-go can save you a lot of time and energy if you ever want to sell.

In my case, I'd been careful to set up tracking codes in my cloud accounting, one for each income stream in my company. Doing this meant I could track all my income and expenses to their relevant tracking codes during the reconciliation process. So, when I wanted a valuation on that single area of the business, it became as simple as clicking a button on a report.

A few days later, my accountant contacted me – not just with a valuation, but with an offer to buy my compliance business.

One month later, he was the new owner.

Of course, much thought went into the sale beforehand, but as I weighed up the pros and cons, I realised I was ready to sell; it was time for me to move out of the day-to-day and embrace the next chapter.

Since then, I'm often asked why I decided to sell and how I knew it was time to move on. There's no simple or single answer, but rather a meeting of preparation and opportunity; some might say luck.

And while I absolutely feel lucky, I also know that the way I set my business up meant that when the opportunity arrived, I was in the fortunate position to take advantage of it.

Rather than answer the much-asked question, 'How will I know when it's time to sell?', here's my answer to a more important question: 'How should you set your business up so you can sell it?'

Here are my tips:

- **Start with an exit plan in mind:** What's the end goal for yourself and your business? Consider the ideal timeframe for selling, the financial target you wish to achieve, and any personal or professional aspirations tied to the sale.

- **Start as you mean to continue:** Always consider what success means to you and build your business accordingly. Business should be about purpose, so what's yours? Intentionally building a solid foundation where you're clear on your vision, mission, and values will make you more likely to attract a potential buyer with similar beliefs. In my case, it was important for me to sell to someone who understood where I was coming from and who intended to look after my clients as I did.

- **Have organised financial records:** Ideally dating back to the start of the business. The need for good, accessible records makes cloud accounting essential; a simple spreadsheet won't cut it. Prospective buyers will want to see your business history in numbers: your income, expenses, profit margin, current phase, and potential. Having everything in one place and up to date makes this simple.

- **Keep up to date with your compliance:** The last thing you want is a significant tax debt hanging over your head because, no matter why you've incurred the debt, it might signal to a prospective buyer that your cash flow and financial systems, processes and habits aren't as good as they could be.

- **Create solid systems and processes and keep them up to date:** Clear and comprehensive standard operating procedures (SOPs) are attractive to prospective buyers because they can help make the business more accessible for the new owner. If they have SOPs they can rely on, they won't need to second-guess or ask 101 questions to operate the business.

- **Customer database:** Documented client records, history and contact information are a must and an asset for your business, and this goes double for your email list or list of potential customers, too. Remember that when you sell, some existing clients will see it as an opportunity to move their business, so having a well-documented and diverse range of clients will allow the new owner to have the best chance of success. Plus, it's just good business!

- **Supplier records and relationships:** Strong relationships with suppliers can positively impact the sale of your business. Nurture your supplier relationships, document any helpful information and include these records in the sale.

MONEY MAGNET TIP:

If you can, sell as a going concern – that means you hand over a complete, operational business. You walk out at 5pm one day, the new owner walks in at 9am the following day, and the business keeps operating. There's no closedown or down time; it's simply a transition from one owner to the next and so seamless that if you didn't mention it to your clients, they'd be none the wiser.

The new owner gets your business name, clients, staff, if they're happy to move across, IP, systems and process, plant or equipment and handover notes if applicable.

Tips for selling your business

- **Sell before it's too late:** If you're thinking of selling your business, be sure to take the steps needed well before you're burnt out or completely 'over-it'. You want to sell at the right time to the right person and for the right money, too.

  Selling because you're tired or fed up might mean that you regret your decision to sell or the terms of the sale further down the track.

- **Be realistic:** So many business owners think their business is worth far more than it's actually worth. So, when it comes time to sell, they're perpetually disappointed by the offers they receive or worse, price their business at such a high value, there are no offers at all.

  While there are many ways to value a business, by far the best way is seeking advice from your accountant or a business broker as the first step.

- **Consult an expert:** If selling might be an option at some point in your business future, talk to an expert in the early stages of business or well before you plan to sell so you have everything ready to go when you decide to proceed.

  Take an honest look at your business. Identify those areas of your business that might be a red flag for a prospective buyer and commit to improving them.

- **Know what's next:** Before I even entertained the thought of selling my business, I wanted to understand where I was headed; what was next for me. I definitely didn't want to be one of those business owners who felt lost and alone when I said goodbye to my business and much-loved clients or whose identity became intertwined with their business.

One of the best things I did presale was to spend time talking about my next chapter. I spoke to family and trusted business friends and by understanding what was next, I found it easier to close one chapter and move on mindfully. And, if you're thinking of selling I'd highly recommend it too.

Chapter 18

Secrets of Successful Business

From Some of My Business Besties

My podcast, Secrets of Successful Business, started back in 2022. I'd been interviewing incredible women and writing their business stories and secrets for years when my kids suggested that podcasting was the way to go because that's what all the cool kids were doing. They even gave me my podcast mic as a birthday present to give me that extra little push.

The podcast is a labour of love and over the years, I've collected a number of business secrets, both from my guests and through chatting to some of my business buddies.

Here's a selection of secrets from some of the best minds in business!

Amy Porterfield's secret

'If you look around and think I'm too late to the game you will not succeed. But if you change your mindset, and that's all entrepreneurship is, I can teach you strategies all day long, but if your mindset is not in the right place, it will not work.'

'The mindset is there is enough room for everyone. No one teaches the way I teach, no one has the experiences or the style of my teaching, I am unique. We are all unique and there are certain people who want to learn from me even though they could learn from ten other people. That's the mindset I want my students to have, knowing there's enough for everyone and there's enough room for you at this table.'

'One of my other secrets to success is that I don't make a lot of pivots. For the last ten years, I have been known for helping people create digital courses. Now, are there some days I talk about this so much that I think, "oh gosh, has this become redundant", and when I feel like that, I find new ways to talk about it, new stories, new strategies, but I stay in my lane.'

'Find your thing and give it more time than you think it needs. Be patient, stay in your lane, don't compare yourself to other people because it never, ever will serve, but if you've got something in you that's special, you deserve to be known for something, to be put on the map for that, but it takes time, so be patient.'

Amy Porterfield is an online marketing expert, host of Online Marketing Made Easy and business owner who sold more than $90M in online courses.

Quote from episode 116 of Secrets of Successful Business Podcast

Lisa Messenger's secret

'Make friends with failure, and know that it's okay!'

'So often in business, we're embarrassed or fearful of failure, or if we fail our egos get bruised, but, failure is good. If you fail, own it authentically, don't shy away from it, but use it to propel you forward.'

'I think that anything is possible. I really believe that because no one is better than anyone else. And if we have that, if we're able to harness that self-belief *in our mindset, even if we fail, I really believe that we can pretty much achieve anything we set our minds to.'*

Lisa Messenger is the founder and CEO of Collective Hub. From print magazines to publishing, Lisa is known as an industry disruptor, thought leader, sought-after global public speaker and best-selling author.

Quote from episode 5 of Secrets of Successful Business Podcast

Alyce Alexandra's secret

'You have to know your why, your mission, and how it all fits together. Know it in your heart beyond "I want to make money". When you come from a place where you want to add value for your client or customer, it's easy to create and sell and talk about your product and why people should invest.'

Alyce Alexandra is the best-selling author of independent cookbooks and accessories for slow-cookers and thermos cooks. Alyce has empowered over 100,000 happy customers to create simple, wholesome food.

Quote from episode 3 of Secrets of Successful Business Podcast

Molly Benjamin's secret

"'If I have any money left at the end of the fortnight, I'll save it." It's no surprise that we never have any money left over at the end of the fortnight. If you don't have a budget, you don't have a plan for your money, and I can guarantee your money will just disappear.'

'Paying yourself first simply means, before you put money away for brunch, groceries, fun stuff, and other expenses, you treat your goals like bills and put the money away first (ideally on payday), and then live on the remaining amount. By setting aside money as soon as you receive your income, you're ensuring your future needs are met and not left up to chance.'

Molly Benjamin is the Founder of Ladies Finance Club and best-selling Author of *Girls Just Wanna have Funds*. Molly does incredible work in the finance space, helping women all over the world increase their financial literacy, particularly in the personal finance space. I'm privileged to be a Ladies Finance Club Ambassador.

Emma Blomfield's secret

'My secret for successful business has been something I ignored for a very long time and felt far too overwhelmed about paying attention to – finances!'

'I relied too much on outsourced help but really should have been across the figures myself to fully understand the financial health of my business. I now set aside time each week and have a digital checklist with a list of bullet points I need to look at or actions relating to things like putting money into the tax account from the takings the week prior, paying the credit card off, reviewing our lead conversion, following up new leads as well as a basic profit and loss review.'

'I've finally learnt to actually enjoy tracking these metrics and find I'm able to make far faster and better commercial decisions for the business because those numbers are front of mind at all times.'

Emma Blomfield is the owner, Director and Principle Stylist of Emma Blomfield Studio. She's also a best-selling Author of three books, Speaker and Business Mentor.

Kate Toon's secret

'A successful business is hugely about mindset. It's the ability to motivate yourself, turn up each day, make a to-do list and then do it. The ability to turn up when things are good or bad, that persistence, and not being on a roller coaster of emotion.'

'It's not taking the good too seriously. Not taking the bad too seriously. But having self-belief and self-confidence, not constantly seeking external affirmation or external education, but having some belief that you already have it within you.'

'For me, mindset has been the most significant thing. You can be the most talented copywriter, the most genius at accounts and the most fabulous graphic designer, but if you don't get your mindset sorted, you'll undo your goodness. You will unpick any beautiful thing you create by worrying away at it.'

Kate Toon is an award-winning business mentor and digital marketing coach, author of the popular business book *'Six Figures in School Hours: How to run a successful business and still be a good parent'.*

Quote from episode 15 of Secrets of Successful Business Podcast

Mel Browne's secret

'Business is an art, business is a science, it's a skill, and the better you can be at business, the better your business will be.'

Mel Browne is an ex-account, ex-financial advisor and author who loves increasing financial literacy and creating financial growth as much as I do.

Quote from episode 54 of Secrets of Successful Business Podcast

Liz Nable's secret

'Accept that you don't know everything and look to those around you who have those skills. From an early stage in business, I felt a bit alone, so I thought, who knows more than me? Who can I ask for help? Who's really smart? Who's a great accountant who can give me advice? Where are these

other men and women running these small businesses, and can I create my own little network? And that's really helped me.'

'Understanding different aspects of the business that were probably not my strengths and accepting or seeking help from people who know more than you do is one of the keys to success.'

Liz Nable is a media and PR expert and known for bringing the Barre franchise to Australia.

Quote from episode 26 of Secrets of Successful Business Podcast

Jen Bishop's secrets

'There's a lot of fluff out there about 6-figure and 7-figure businesses and how to become one, but what people should really be talking about is profit. Vanity aside, it doesn't matter if you have a multi-million-dollar revenue business if you're not profitable.'

Jen Bishop is the Founder and Publisher of The Interiors Addict, an online publication offering the latest interiors, decorating and renovating news. Jen's also an innovator, loyal supporter and champion of women in business!

Maha Corbett's secret

'Success is about a few things, but one of those is understanding what makes money and what doesn't. We learned this the hard way. You can have a lot of different products or offer many different services, but they don't all necessarily make money, and if they don't make money, then what you've got is a hobby; you don't have a business.'

'Understanding pricing and margins and how much money you're going to end up with at the end of the day after all of your costs are taken out is

critical. It sounds obvious, but in the early days, it's more complicated than it sounds.'

'When we started the SWIISH, our online store, we'd price things based on what we thought someone would want to pay for a product without really factoring in what we were paying to procure the item, the cost to ship it or how much our overheads, insurance and other expenses were. It sounds mad when I say it out loud, and I wonder why we didn't know that sooner.'

'We had a big mishmash of products, and it wasn't easy to see which parts of the business were making money and which weren't. Initially, we thought, oh, we're doing amazing, but in reality, there were certain products or certain areas that were loss-making, and they were a real drainer.'

'It was only by separating all of those revenue streams that we were able to say, well, that's not working. Okay. We've got to change or stop that.'

'The other thing I wish that I knew is that everything takes so much longer than you think it's going to take; whether it's product development, collecting cash from a customer, or building an online business, everything takes longer than you think, so consider that right from the start.'

Maha Corbett is the Co-Founder of SWIISH, one of Australia's leading wellness and beauty brands. Founded in 2012 with her sister Sally Obermeder, the SWIISH philosophy is all about being undeniably you.

Quote from episode 22 of Secrets of Successful Business Podcast

Colleen Callander's secret

'A successful business is about knowing your values and believing in yourself. But there are a couple of really clear things that are super important outside of that. You need to know your brand pitch and why you exist and then build real emotional connections with your customers that go beyond what you sell.'

'People don't want to be sold to; most people want to connect with brands. So, how does your brand differentiate? How do I create meaning in my customer's life? It doesn't matter whether you're a small business or a big business. I really challenge you to think about why you're here and what the problem you're trying to solve in your customer's life is or how you're trying to serve her differently.'

'The other really big one is that having a clear vision is key, but there's a really big difference between having a vision and having people who want to follow your vision. I always say a vision is great, and you need it, but people follow a leader. So, if you're not a leader that people want to follow, it doesn't matter how damn good your vision is; it doesn't matter how well you stand up and sell it to people.'

'At the end of the day, it all has to do with the people, whether they believe in you as the leader, whether they know that you're going to be there to pick them when they fall over because when they know you're going to let them take risks and it's going to be okay when they make a mistake, they're the kind of leaders that people want to follow and that I think is part of business success.'

Colleen Callander is a Former CEO, Founder of Mentor Me Women, Author, Speaker and Business Advisor.

Quote from episode of 36 Secrets of Successful Business Podcast

Anita Siek's secret

'Consistency! It's consistency in all different business areas, whether in content, messaging or how you show up.'

'It's about looking at every single interaction you have with your audience and always listening, learning, showing up and being present; that's what builds a brand and a business as well.'

Anita Siek, founder and owner of Wordfetti, helps business owners zig when others zag. Anita is a brand, communication and copywriting specialist.

Quote from episode 7 of Secrets of Successful Business Podcast

Chapter 19

Your Financial Success Journey

'Don't be intimidated by what you don't know. That can be your greatest strength and ensure that you do things differently from everyone else.'

Sara Blakely, Founder of Spanx

Balance is where effort meets ease, so as you embark on your financial success journey, the trick is to find that place for you.

Getting your finances in order and putting yourself in that balanced position may take a lot of work initially. However, when you start to embed some of the habits and sound financial practices mentioned in this book, when you put in the effort, one thing I know for sure is that it will get easier.

And, like anything, the more you do, the better you'll get, the less effort you'll need to put in, and the easier it will become. Before you know it, you'll become a business money magnet™ and have more money in your personal life, too.

But remember, no matter where you're starting from, there is always a price for the next level of success. That price could be fear, time, money, ego, or relationships; it could be reframing what success looks like for you or completely reconsidering how your business works. When you are intentional about every choice you make in your business, in your life, and with your money going forward, you are fully in the driver's seat. Although there's always a price to pay, you get to choose your adventure and the upside; there will always be personal and professional growth.

As you start or continue on your financial success journey, here are some things to remember.

- Your success starts with you deciding on your **unique success destination**, one that suits this season of your life and your business. Once you choose, live it and empower yourself to achieve your goals.

- It's never too late or too early; you're never too old, too young, or too set in your ways to make a change, but if you want to achieve financial success and design the life you love, you **need to start**!

- As you kick off your journey, no matter where you're starting from, there will be bumps and hiccups along the way; I guarantee it. **The key to success is resilience!** It's about taking a step back when things don't go your way and starting again with the benefit of hindsight. Because even though you might not think it at the time, there'll be a valuable lesson in that bump in the road or in that challenge.

- **Nothing is ever wasted!** Everything you've done so far in life is a building block to help you reach the next destination in your journey. You might not understand or even value it at the time, but as you look back, you'll see how that thing you learned, a random encounter or an experience prepared you for this next stage.

- **Overwhelm will happen**, especially when it comes to money. It's natural and can lead to poor mental and physical health, so don't keep pushing when things aren't going your way. Instead, **stop, review, rest, refresh and start again**.

- **Not everyone will be on your side, and that's okay**. A successful business is not the destination for everyone. It takes a particular person to step out of their comfort zone and choose a business journey, and often, those non-entrepreneurial people won't understand you or what you want to achieve. So ...

- **Trust yourself!** It's as simple as that.

- **Embrace your strengths** and outsource to save you time and money. Get help when needed; it's often the fastest way to get where you want to go.

- **Value yourself**; value your skill set, time, energy, and always, always price for profit!

- It doesn't have to be complicated – **put in the effort and then find the ease**; that's where balance comes in.

- Finance might not be the sexiest part of your business, but when you've got a handle on the numbers, it means there's lots of possibilities and opportunities ahead. As I always say to my kids, it's important to **leave all the doors open**. In other words, as you move forward in life, learn what you can because knowledge is powerful and can never be taken away from you. Knowledge also means choice, and choice can lead to opportunity, a place where all the doors are always open for you to walk through.

- While on your journey, **be kind to every person you meet** along the way. Try not to burn bridges because you never know when you might need to knock on that door again, and when you do, you want it to swing wide open.

- Remember **that your numbers tell a story**, and you owe it to yourself to be the author of your own story! Don't let someone else write your beginning, middle or end.

- **Consistency wins every time!** So, what's a one percent improvement you can make today and every day in your business? Those little steps will add up to significant progress, and it's the only way to achieve those big goals.

No matter what you think about money, where you are on your business journey or what anyone else tells you, let me be the one to say that you've got this and you've had the power all along!

As you work through this book, empower yourself with financial know-how and begin the process of tidying up and improving your finances and you will start to see results. Small changes will lead to big progress and turn you into a formidable business money magnet^{TM}.

And, if you ever feel like giving up, swing back and read chapter one, my story, over again. Because that gal who 'didn't do numbers' all those years ago, not only managed to turn around a business in debt, but also created a business that she sold for a profit and now has choices.

Choice: the freedom to decide your next step is life-changing, and I want that for you.

Numbers tell a story and none more than your business numbers – so, choose to be the author of your story – make it epic and give yourself the freedom of choice!

Until we meet again, here's to you living your unique success journey and becoming a magnificent, business money magnet™!

I'd love to connect, so reach out on Instagram @flossifiles, LinkedIn or come visit us at https://www.justinemclean.com. Or use the QR code to grab the book resources in one easy place.

Extra Resources

Business Money Magnet™

Business Money Magnet™ is Justine's signature program and includes:

- 12 months membership.

- Eight business money modules so you can learn at your own pace.

- Regular weekly group coaching sessions over the 12-month membership.

- Bonus modules, masterclasses and workshops with Justine and guest experts.

- A closed Facebook Community Group.

- Templates, checklists and so much more.

For more information or to join google Business Money Magnet™ or head to https://www.justinemclean.com/bmm-sales and use the code BOOK20 to get a reader discount.

Government Support

Australia:
https://business.gov.au/

NZ:
https://www.business.govt.nz/

USA:
https://home.treasury.gov/policy-issues/small-business-programs/smal
l-and-disadvantaged-business-utilization/small-business-resources

UK:
https://www.gov.uk/browse/business

EU:
https://europa.eu/youreurope/business/index_en.htm

Asia-Pacific:
https://www.apec.org/about-us/about-apec/business-resources

Also, check your state and local government websites for assistance, free education grants, taxation and other business tools.

Book Resources

To get your free resources mentioned throughout the book, simply go here https://www.justinemclean.com/book-resources or use the QR code below.

Acknowledgements

Writing a book has been on my bucket list even before I knew what a bucket list was, so this book feels like a full-circle moment.

First, I want to thank Sarah and Toby at The Rural Publishing Company for taking a chance on me as a first-time author and running with this book. Thank you also to their team for their work in producing this book and creating incredible cover art. Rachel Tribout for bringing my magnet person to life despite my strange request for shoes and hands, and Jade Warne and Emma Lovell for the awesome back cover photo.

A massive thank you to Sarah Megginson, who helped me polish my book proposal, painstakingly read every word of the manuscript and helped me improve it before submitting it.

To Kate Toon, a huge supporter of my book-writing journey – thank you for sharing all the behind-the-scenes book secrets and for writing such lovely things about my book. Legend!

Kerry Rowett and Shannah Kennedy, thank you for answering my questions and contributing your thoughts and expertise to the book – I appreciate your help.

Rebecca Saunders, business BFF, supporter, and CCO (Chief Celebration Officer) – thank you for always being in my corner, your friendship and fab ideas!

Amy Byrne and Laura Robinson, I appreciate your comments, suggestions and messages about the book. You're my ideal readers, and this book aims to help small business owners like you. Thank you for helping me make the book as useful as possible.

To the Flossi Community, my clients, past and present and my business buddies, I appreciate you and all the cheerleading from the sidelines.

To my readers, I hope this book has demystified business money and inspired you to strive for your business goals, make the money you deserve, and become business money magnets^{TM}!

Finally, to my incredible family.

David, who encouraged me to do this book, read every word and discussed every idea, concept and thought I had while I pulled it together. Thank you for encouraging me to take on this project and helping me get it out into the world. I couldn't have done it without you. I love you!

And our boys, Ben, Lachy, Ryan and Jackson – who have only known their mum as a business owner. I started in business so I could spend more time with you, and along the way, you've taught me so much about life, business and striving for what you want. I'm in absolute awe of everything you have achieved and can't wait to see the places you'll go. I love you!

Last, but not least, thank you to Joseph Kenworthy, my sister from another mister, you are the very best, love you my friend.

About the Author

Justine McLean

Justine McLean is a respected mentor, author, speaker and financial educator on a mission to help business owner's increase their financial literacy, build solid financial foundations and create profitable and sustainable businesses.

With 30 years of experience in small business – retail, e-commerce, publishing and financial services – Justine is sought-after for her practical, tailored and proactive approach to business; clients describe Justine as 'the nice warm hug your business finances need'.

A registered BAS agent, host of the Secrets of Successful Business podcast and Ladies Finance Club Ambassador, Justine was named one of the Coach Foundation's Top Female Business Coaches for 2022.

References

1. Gunderson EA, Gripshover SJ, Romero C, Dweck CS, Goldin-Meadow S, Levine SC. . *Child Dev.* 2013;84(5):1526-1541. doi:10.1111/cdev.1 2064

2. Kendall's Money Personality quiz: https://www.sacredmoneyarche types.com/quiz/

3. https://www.abs.gov.au/statistics/economy/business-indicators/co unts-australian-businesses-including-entries-and-exits/latest-releas e

4. U.S. Small Business Administration Office of Advocacy

5. https://quickbooks.intuit.com/au/blog/news/

6. The Household, Income and Labour Dynamics in Australia (HILDA) Survey 2016

7. https://hbswk.hbs.edu/archive/the-economics-of-e-loyalty